A Beginner's Guide to Charting Financial Markets

Financial Markets

A practical introduction to technical analysis for investors

by Michael Kahn

HARRIMAN HOUSE LTD

3A Penns Road
Petersfield
Hampshire
GU32 2EW
GREAT BRITAIN

Tel: +44 (0)1730 233870
Fax: +44 (0)1730 233880
Email: enquiries@harriman-house.com
Website: www.harriman-house.com

First published in Great Britain in 2007 by Harriman House.

Copyright © Harriman House Ltd

The right of Michael Khan to be identified as the author has been asserted
in accordance with the Copyright, Design and Patents Act 1988.

ISBN 1-905-641-21-4

978-1-905641-21-5

British Library Cataloguing in Publication Data
A CIP catalogue record for this book can be obtained from the British Library.

Charts used with permission of eSignal
Index by Indexing Specialists (UK) Ltd
Printed and bound in Great Britain by William Clowes Ltd, Beccles, Suffolk

This book is dedicated to small investors everywhere

Contents

About the author

Michael N. Kahn currently writes the twice-weekly column "Getting Technical" for *Barron's Online*. He also produces a daily technical market newsletter, *Quick Takes Pro*, (www.QuickTakesPro.com).

Previously, he was chief technical analyst for BridgeNews, a division of Bridge Information Systems.

He has been a regular guest on the *Nightly Business Report* on PBS, has appeared on CNBC and was the editor of the Market Technicians Association newsletter *Technically Speaking*. His first book, *Real World Technical Analysis*, was published in January 1998, and his second, *Technical Analysis: Plain and Simple*, is now in its second edition (2006) and is published in several languages.

Prior to writing technical commentary, Mr. Kahn was a senior product manager for Knight-Ridder Financial before that company was merged into Bridge. He was responsible for the marketing design of several of the firm's charting software platforms and launched technical analysis coverage for Knight-Ridder Financial News. He was also a co-editor of the *Tradecenter Market Letter*.

Prior to joining Bridge/Knight-Ridder Financial in 1986, Mr. Kahn was a senior municipal bond specialist with Merrill Lynch. He also worked in the Financial Planning Department at Shearson Lehman American Express.

Mr. Kahn holds a Bachelor of Arts in Physics and Economics from Brandeis University and a Master of Business Administration from New York University. He is also working on his Chartered Market Technician professional designation.

Preface

Who this is for

If you've always wondered about charts and how they can help you make better investment decisions, then this book is for you. Without using any jargon or complicated formulas, we'll just focus on making the only decision there is to make when it comes to the markets – buy, sell or hold.

What the book contains

We're not focusing on squeezing that last nickel out of a stock. We're not paving a path towards becoming a professional trader or even a trader at all. All we want to do is take whatever analysis we have already done, whether it is based on earnings, demographic trends or interest rates, and make it better. We know what we think of a stock. Let's find out what the market thinks and that's where charts excel.

At the end of the day, if our analysis is sound and the charts agree, then we can be confident with our decisions. If the charts disagree, then perhaps we should move on to our second choice or even just stay away from the market altogether. In any case, we will gain a sense of confidence and that is worth a lot.

How the book is structured

This book is in two parts, the first laying the groundwork and the second putting that knowledge to the test. One theme the reader will notice is that we are searching for the spirit of the analysis and are not concerned with precision and picky details. After all, no matter how fancy the indicators and how complex the maths behind any investment system, the bottom line is answering the question: "Do we buy it or not?"

Introduction

This book is about arming investors with one simple tool that will enhance the investment decision-making process – the chart.

It is not the Holy Grail and even if applied exactly as offered there is no guarantee that the reader will be successful. But owning a high quality hammer is no guarantee that the user will build a beautiful house. The hammer is a tool and in most cases the user will still need other tools – and knowledge – to build that house.

Despite its enormous and still growing popularity, technical market analysis still gets a bad rap. Purveyors of this art have been called tealeaf readers, and many similar names, but that has nothing to do with what technical analysis is attempting to do. If we strip away all the fancy indicators and obtuse jargon, what is left is a time-tested method of finding investment opportunities and assessing their risk. There is no fortune-telling here; only figuring out what we can do about the market. And what we do is the only part of the markets that we can control.

What this book will do is give the reader the basics needed to look at a chart and get a feel for what the market or individual stock is doing. It will cover only the nuts and bolts of chart analysis, barely touching upon the next level concepts, and definitely leaving the whiz-bang stuff well alone.

It should be stressed that this book will not replace the reader's current methods of stock selection and investment strategies. What it can do, however, is add a new dimension to the analysis to confirm or refute what is already known. Basically, there is no need to give up other methods for selecting stocks, although by the end of the book the reader may be drawn to further learning and eventually discover that charts can, indeed, be the primary, if not sole, investment decision-making tools.

Some notes:

The terms *charting* and *technical analysis* are nearly interchangeable for the purposes of this book. The latter may bring connotations of more advanced concepts but don't let that worry you. This book is written for beginners.

The focus of the book is on the stock market with occasional references to others, such as bonds or commodities. Charts are completely comfortable operating in any market so everything covered here applies to the individual investor in any country where there are developed markets.

The reader will notice that chapters overlap each other and many concepts and analyses are introduced and reintroduced, sometimes several times. This is by design to hammer home certain points and allow each chapter to stand alone.

So let's get into it and discover a new world of investing tools that are sure to open a few eyes and make the process a little bit easier.

1

Introduction To Charting

There are many different types of charts but the simplest to comprehend at the beginner level are those that plot price action over time. For our purposes in this book we will only consider two main types of charts:

1. one summarizes a period's trading, called *bar charts*, and

2. one simply connects the close prices together to form a line, not surprisingly called *close charts* or *line charts*.

A period can be a single day, a week, a year, or a unit of 10 minutes. All of them are made in the same way and the only difference is the time horizon in which each operates. As beginners, let's keep to daily and weekly charts.

1. The Basics Of Chart Reading

What is a chart?

A chart is a tool both investors and traders use to help them determine whether to buy or sell a stock, a bond, commodity or a currency. In one neat package, a huge amount of data can be viewed and as they say:

A picture is worth a thousand words.

For investors, that picture can be worth a thousand days of data, or a thousand weeks of data with, if one chooses, as many indicators and formulas as one can fathom.

As mentioned, bar charts summarize all the trading for any given time period, such as a day or a week (see Chart 1.1). When all those summaries are plotted together, trends emerge and patterns form – all revealing where a stock is right now and how it got there. After all, knowing a stock is trading at a price of 50 is not of much help, but knowing it was at 45 last month and 40 the month before gives us a good idea that it has been in a bullish trend.

Chart 1.1

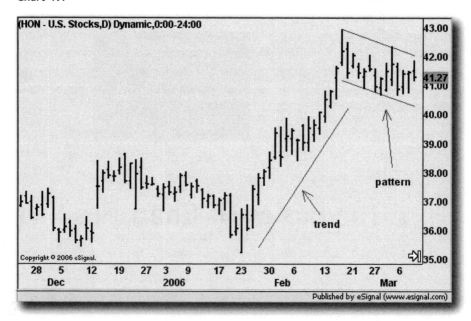

Some analysts look at a chart and simply draw an arrow on the actual data plot. If the arrow is pointing up, they know the trend is up. Conversely, if the arrow is pointing down, they know the trend is down.

Of course, sometimes the arrow points sideways and other times it is not clear where the arrow should go. That will be addressed later in this book, but suffice it to say there will be times when the charts don't help in making the decision to buy, sell or hold. That's fine. No tool can be applied on all projects. A hammer is a valuable tool for a carpenter but it cannot turn a screw or loosen a plumbing connection, and the same applies to any tool investors may choose to use.

A brief history of charting

Chart watching can trace its roots back more than 200 years to Japanese rice trading. Charles Dow, a forefather of modern technical analysis, and a co-founder of Dow Jones & Co., made his ground-breaking observations in the late nineteenth century.

Analysis was done with paper and pencil for decades until personal computers made their appearance, and with these the sophistication of the analysis blossomed.

Over the past 20 years or so, charting has spread from a few Wall Street analysts with access to price and volume data to the mainstream. With the explosion of trading activity by individuals in the 1990s, the markets became incredibly liquid and technical analysis was perfectly suited to take advantage of the activity. But as computer power became cheaper and websites offering free tools and cheap trade execution became prevalent, market volume – and volatility – soared.

Price movements that previously occurred over periods of months were occurring weekly and this required chart watchers to adapt their tools to the new market situation.

Whereas price patterns or ranges on the charts used to be small in relation to the stock price, such as a two-point range on a $25 stock (8%), these same ranges became much larger, such as a five-point range on that same stock (20%).

Breakouts still occurred but price movements following those moves were faster and stronger to create conditions where investors had to anticipate breakouts in order not to be left at the starting gate.

> A good rule of thumb is to restrict technical analysis to stocks that trade at least 100,000 shares per day so that there is a liquid market for the stock.

With the proliferation of online trading, charting has fallen victim of its own success as investors are forced to break the rules of analysis to get the jump on others. Everyone knows about the adage, "Sell in May and go away" so they begin to sell in April to get a beat on the crowd. The so-called "Santa Claus rally" is used to describe the seasonal tendency for stocks to move higher at the end of the year, but this phenomenon has already started to occur a month sooner. The reasons are the same. It's just that investors are trying to be first in and first out so the whole process is played out earlier.

Because of this, it can be said that analysis of the market as a whole has changed drastically. However, there is a happy medium between the over-analysed market and highly risky penny stocks where individual investors can comfortably make money without resorting to guesswork.

A good rule of thumb is to restrict technical analysis to stocks that trade at least 100,000 shares per day so that there is a liquid market for the stock. Maintain a watch on the overall market to keep the overall trend in mind, because there are too many highly paid and highly skilled professionals focusing on what the Standard & Poor's 500 is going to do. That reduces any advantage enjoyed by small investors in the past.

What is the market?

The market – any market – has been personified by both the media and by investors. "What did the market do?" a friend asks.

Investors, analysts and journalists treat the market as a living, breathing entity. "The market did not like the latest employment report," they might say. Or "the market was energized by Company X's positive reaction".

But just who, or what, is the market?

The market is simply the sum of the actions of everyone in it. There is no one, central brain controlling things, nor is there any agenda to move one way or the other.

Crowd psychology

There is, however, a collective consciousness as people in the market buy and sell in reaction to their own analysis and the actions of others as they, in turn, buy and sell. Many liken the market to a herd of animals, a flock of birds or a school of fish.

If a fish on the right side of a school sees a shark approaching, its action causes a ripple effect through the whole school; and fish all the way on the left side – despite not seeing the shark themselves – start to veer to the left. Information about the presence of the shark propagates through the school much the same as information about a company propagates through the market. The school and the market somehow start to move as a unit. For the market, that is a *trend*.

What charts can do

Charts merely display information in graphical form so that patterns and trends come alive on the screen and bring out the meaning in the market. They reveal actions of the crowd and they allow the user to quickly spot where the market may encounter problems or where it presents a good risk to take.

Think of it this way; an athlete can read a textbook and time his or her performance, but a video can break down each move and hone in on where improvements can be made. Technology is more sensitive, more accurate and much faster in terms of gathering data and rendering it into a useful form than human senses and brains. The latter two are critical for interpretation, but for sheer data gathering and number crunching power, charts are unparalleled.

Here is another analogy: the simple act of walking. You don't think about it, you just do it. Your mind and body have it all figured out and ready to use. Charts take market information, figure out the patterns and then give them to you to use.

What is a trend?

Patterns and trends have already been mentioned, so let's quickly talk about them so confusion does not set in.

In simplest terms:

- a *trend* is the market in motion, and

- a *pattern* is the market at rest, deciding if it wants to continue its trend or change course.

We'll talk more about patterns later, after we nail down some of the basic concepts of charting first.

A trend is really nothing more than a somewhat uniform change in price levels over time. For a rising, or bull trend, prices start low and through a series of fits and starts, advances and pullbacks, move to a higher level. Some trends are smooth and have small wiggles within. Others are choppy and are characterized by high volatility. Some are flat with little net gain over time, and others are steep with a sharp increase in relatively little time.

The basic point about all trends, however, is that they have inertia. Trends in motion tend to stay in motion until an outside force acts upon them. And how do they get inertia? It is from the imperfect flow of information.

According to the followers of the Random Walk theory (see page 12), everything that is known is priced into a stock and only when new information comes out can a stock move. Under that scenario, stock prices must move only in quantum leaps. Stock X is trading at 40 the day before positive earnings news and should then jump to 42, for example, after the news, where it should stay until the next bit of news becomes known.

We all know that this does not happen in the real world. Somebody knows something or thinks they know something and buys. The next person notices the buying and decides to buy as well. Information about both the company and trading in its stock spreads around the marketplace, where different people learn about and absorb the news at different rates. Prices gradually move from 40 to 42, and sometimes even to 43 as exuberance (greed) in the market takes it past presumed value.

Supply and demand

There are price levels on the chart that investors consider to be cheap or expensive. In chart lingo, that is *support* and *resistance*, respectively.

Resistance slows or stops a trend. Support holds the market from falling further, at least temporarily. But in reality, it is supply and demand, respectively. Sellers, for example, become more aggressive when they think prices are high and they sell. That increases supply and prices will ease lower unless demand also increases.

For example, if a price of 50 for a stock brought out the sellers on one or two occasions in the recent past, this price level is considered to be *resistance*, where the supply of stock increases relative to the demand. People think it is expensive so they attempt to sell. Simple economic theory suggests that prices will stop going up, if not actually decline.

Perhaps the stock declines to 45, where buyers think it is cheap. Prices begin to edge higher and this process repeats until something changes the perception of the stock's value, either from inside the market (attitudes and outlooks of investors) or outside the market (earnings and politics). At that point, a price of 50 may suddenly look cheap and demand overwhelms supply. The stock then moves higher.

The spirit of the market

Any market, from stocks to bonds to groceries, is designed to match supply with demand and it does so by adjusting price. And it does so automatically, as each person acts to maximize his or her own value – selling for as much as possible or buying for as little as possible within tolerances for quality, risk and other intangibles.

When taken in this way, the market does seem to come alive, but it is no more alive than any other social system. It is, however, the sum of the actions of all

> Real values do not change 20% in a day, but perceptions of that value sure can.

investors and in that way it does seem to have a mind of its own.

If a stock appears more valuable because the company announced a new customer deal, then people will buy it until it no longer appears quite as valuable. Actual value, defined by any method we choose, rarely matches market value, if ever. Perceptions of stock prices swing from cheap to expensive. Attitudes in the market swing from extreme pessimism to extreme optimism.

How else can we explain a bubble? Or a crash? Real values do not change 20% in a day, but perceptions of that value sure can.

It is the best way to separate market value from market perception and note when the latter is changing. The former does not move prices. Only the latter does.

 Charts detail the day-to-day, or even minute-to-minute, changes in what people think something is worth.

Styles of market analysis

There are several methods used by investors and professional money managers to construct their investment portfolios. It is also fair to say that most people do not employ one method exclusively, preferring to get a check from another discipline to verify their conclusions. The secret is to find where one's own style and comfort level lies within the diagram in Figure 1.1.

Figure 1.1

Styles of Market Analysis

Fundamental analysis – the study of earnings, revenues, business pipelines and strategies – is the predominant method used to analyse stocks. The theory is that the analyst can find a valuation for the company and thereby determine if the shares are under- or overvalued. From there, the buy, sell or hold recommendation is made.

Some may also group economic and quantitative analysis together with fundamental analysis. In both economic and fundamental analysis there is a large degree of forecasting of the data used to create the stock forecast. In other words, next year's earnings and the current quarter's economic report are both best guesses. How many times do we see an economic report revised later – well after any investment decision based on it has been made?

Many individual investors are raised to believe that the stock market will always go up over time and that it is futile to time buys and sells. That is the basis for the random walk theory and a book, *A Random Walk Down Wall Street*, by Burton Malkiel, first published in 1973. His conclusion was that investors couldn't time the market.

Another bit of faulty investor logic is the expected average annual return for stocks of 10% or more. What most people forget is that 10% is an average return. If the stock market was rising at 20% per year during the bubble years of the late 1990s, then there are going to be lean years where the return in the stock market is smaller – and some years when it will actually be negative.

If you followed a buy and hold strategy in early 2000, before the bear market began, then it took seven years for the stock market to return to break-even. That is a 0% return for seven years, and why some call the buy and hold strategy "buy and hope".

The final area of analysis, the one you are reading this book to learn, is technical analysis.

 Technical analysis is based solely on data generated by the market and by the actions of people in the market. Data are never revised later. Analysts are not making guesses on the value of the data.

Technical analysis focuses on how stock prices are moving and how powerful those moves are. By analysing these two simple data sets – price and volume – it creates derivative measures, such as momentum, and all of it is used to ultimately measure supply and demand. These are the forces that really move markets and not analyst estimates or government reports. If nobody demands what is being supplied, no matter how great the fundamentals look, then prices are not going to go up.

These are not mysterious concepts and certainly not what some paint technical analysis to be. All we want to do is figure out where the market is going, hop on board for the ride and then hopefully recognize when the market is changing its mind in time for us to hop back off.

In recent years, two related fields – behavioural analysis

Supply and demand. These are the forces that really move markets and not analyst estimates or government reports.

and socionomics – have gained followings. Both analyse market action with quantifiable actions of people and add great insights.

- *Behavioural finance* studies how people act when money is at stake.

- *Socionomics* looks at the social mood in society and relates it back to what the stock market is doing.

However, this book will focus just on more traditional technical analysis and leave it to the reader to explore the others at a later date.

Why charts matter

Technical analysis is a bit of a misnomer since it's not that technical. Sure, there are some complex mathematical concepts tied to it but, at its core, technical analysis is simply a method of determining if a stock, or the market as a whole, is going up or going down. Once we identify these trends, and that is something we can do by simply looking at a chart, we are way ahead of the game with regard to assembling a winning portfolio.

Just why do charts work?

In order to understand how to invest in any market, it is important to understand what drives the market in the first place. Many cite fundamentals as the force behind moves in the stock market, and that is true to a degree. However, as mentioned earlier, it is not value that determines price, it is perception of value. And when does anything ever trade at fair value? If it did, then fundamental analysts would all be out of work, as the market would always tell us what a stock is worth.

This was mentioned earlier but it deserves a reprise: No matter what new products a company invents or how much it beat analyst earnings estimates, if nobody wants to buy its stock at the current price then its stock price will not go up. And what determines if an investor wants to buy anything? Perceptions.

If Joe Investor does not think that prices will move higher on the latest news, brokerage recommendation or because interest rates just went up, and there are enough Joe Investors of like mind, then prices will indeed *not* move higher. But, as can be inferred from this statement, there must be a critical mass of Joe Investors with the same perceptions. Any market is dependent on the crowd, for it is crowd psychology behind market perceptions (see page 8).

Sometimes one investor wants to buy a stock simply because everyone else has bought it. Where else would a rational person wait to buy something until it had a higher price? While we will see later in this book that this sort of thinking can lead to success, it cannot be employed without looking at the charts to see if there are any surprises waiting.

One look at the next chart illustrates this point. In April 2004, Microsoft announced very good earnings and the stock jumped up (see Chart 1.2). After all, the fundamentals were good and everyone else thought it was a good buy.

However, at the new price there were many investors waiting to unload shares they had from purchases made the last time the stock rallied in late 2003.

How do we know that?

The patterns on the chart tell us. Each time the stock tags the top of its pattern it falls, so it is a good bet that it will happen again.

So, despite the temporary euphoria surrounding the company, the perceived value of the stock did not change. As the air was let out of the balloon, investors sold more and prices sagged back to where they were before.

Chart 1.2

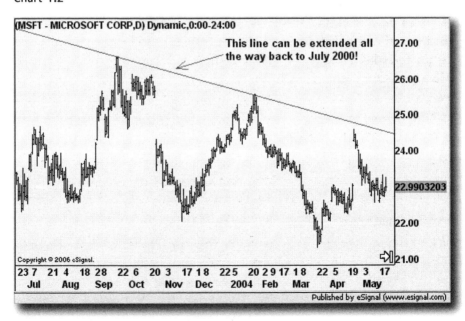

What are we really trying to do here?

All the mathematical calculations and computer programs used by professional traders are great tools – if you are moving huge amounts of money in and out of the market. What individual investors really need to know is whether they should be in the market, and if so what they should buy. It's that simple.

What we are really trying to do here is understand the mood of the market:

- Is it happy or not?

- Is one sector in favour over another?

- Are there any warnings signs we need to know?

Much of this is covered in more detail in Part II of this book, *Putting Charts To Work For You.*

But it all boils down to making a decision to buy, sell or hold. We'll look a bit more into this in the chapter: *Putting Stocks To The Technical Test.*

The focus is on action, not prediction. We cannot control where the market will go tomorrow or next year but we can control what we do to prepare for it – and includes knowing when we have made an incorrect assessment.

> The focus is on action, not prediction.

So what is technical analysis?

- Crowd psychology
- The herd
- Probabillity
- Fear and greed
- Supply and demand

As mentioned earlier, technical analysis is based solely on data generated by the market and by the actions of people in the market. It is based on the premise that people will act in similar ways when faced with similar conditions.

But to be more pragmatic, it is a tool used to make investment decisions. It helps assess risk and reward. And it can assist investors in allocating their resources among stocks, sectors and asset classes. Wouldn't a tool to help decide what portion of a portfolio should be devoted to stocks, bonds, cash and a hard asset such as gold be quite valuable?

Charts are where perception meets reality. A stock may look cheap according to an analyst's calculations based on projected future earnings, but if there is no demand for the stock it is simply not going to go up. A stock is only worth what people think it is worth, not what it should be worth on paper.

And what about those projected earnings?

Again, as mentioned earlier, they are really only educated guessed about the future business success used to make educated guesses about price action in the future. That's two degrees of guesses – educated or not.

On the charts, we look at what is happening right now and how it came to be. From there we make educated guesses about the future; but the goal is not to predict where prices will be in a year. The real goal is to determine what we do about it right now. If we decide to buy based on a chart, we will already know what has to happen to prove us wrong and that helps us limit losses.

> Charts are where perception meets reality.

As prices fell during the bear market of the early 2000s, stocks that were undervalued based on the fundamentals got even more undervalued, at least initially before the declining market took its toll on the economy. Technical analysts recognized the declining trend early and took their losses right away, making it difficult to find competent chart readers that rode stocks all the way down. They recognized a bear market as it was happening and not after businesses suffered enough to change earnings estimates.

For example, an analyst upgraded the stock of Hewlett-Packard to a *strong buy* with a one-year price target of $40 in June of 2001 (see Chart 1.3). But it continued to fall for months simply because the trend – the bear market, in this case – was down. The market was speaking!

Chart 1.3

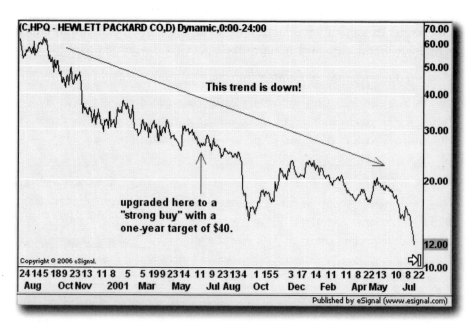

Note that all technical analysts did during the bear market was look at one simple portion of the chart – price action. Despite what we think about a stock or a market, what we see is what counts. For Hewlett-Packard, we see a bear market and in three month's time the stock was down over 40%. While this is obviously a dramatic example, it is not unusual at all. And we did not use any fancy indicators or formulas to analyse it, either.

With that said, this is not an admonishment of fundamental analysis, which is a valuable part of the investment decision-making process in terms of finding quality companies and avoiding those that are in trouble. But that does not tell us what the market is thinking and that is where technical analysis shines.

What technical analysis is not

Some detractors liken technical analysis to voodoo or tealeaf reading, which might be true if the absolute goal is to predict the future. But nobody and no method can do that. What technical analysis tries to do is assess the probability of prices moving one way or the other so we can take action. We may be wrong but, over time, playing probabilities will pan out as a good strategy.

Briefly, technical analysis is not predicting the future or an endorsement or criticism of any company. There is an element of prediction as it attempts to find the probability of future action. There is an element of judgement about a company but it is its stock – not the company itself – that is under scrutiny. Sometimes the stock of a most excellent company can be priced so high as to make it a poor investment.

Why use it?

A logical question is:

> What does technical analysis do for me?

The answer is that the ability to recognize when a stock has reached a support or resistance level, or a shift in perceptions takes place, can help investors know whether to use the:

- *buy low, sell high* approach, or
- *buy high, sell higher* approach, or
- whether to buy the stock at all.

The ability to apply this one aspect of chart reading will reveal the market to investors with the same impact as understanding the colours of a traffic light. Once you know that green means go and red means stop, you will know when it is safe to buy or not.

We've touched upon some of the reasons to use technical analysis, such as the lack of data revisions, estimates and subjectivity in its inputs. But as important as it is to know when to buy a stock it is equally, if not more, important to know when not to buy a stock, or when to sell a stock already held. Technical analysis is the only investment decision-making discipline that lets you know when you are wrong sooner, rather than later, to minimize losses.

When not to use it?

Since technical analysis is based on crowd psychology and actions of the masses, it works best when there is a crowd to analyse. That means the best analysis occurs on liquid stocks where there are plenty of bulls and bears at work and a critical mass of money value changes hands each day. What constitutes critical mass is subjective, but many investors use a rule of thumb of stock price above $20 and average daily trading volume above 100,000 shares. Certainly we can tinker with these parameters as we gain experience.

Technical analysis also needs relatively normal market conditions. War, terrorism, takeovers, legislation and litigation trump support and resistance, although it does help during these unusual conditions to know where investors found value in the past.

2. How To Read A Chart

This section is not about how to use charting and technical analysis but rather it is a simple introduction to what is on a chart and what to do with it. There is a lot of information packed into even the simplest of charts, but the most important can be spotted quickly with just a few guidelines. Think of this section as a Quick Start guide.

The basic parts of a chart

Most charts have a main area where prices are plotted. Some have indicators plotted in a sub-window either above or below the main area, some have supporting data plotted as an overlay on prices and, of course, some have both. Chart 2.1 is a typical arrangement of both an overlay (moving averages, in this case) and an indicator (volume).

Chart 2.1

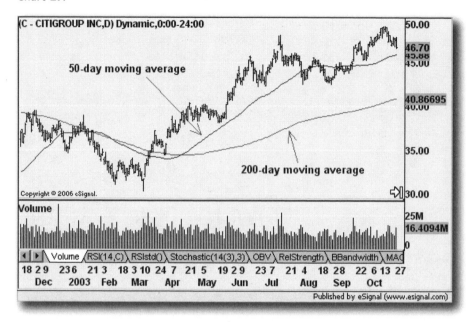

Price bars

Most charts plot price action on the vertical axis and time on the horizontal axis (see Chart 2.1). There are charts that plot price action without regard to time (such as *point and figure* and *point break* charts), but these are best left to specialized books on other chart types. This book will focus on price vs. time charts with an emphasis on bar charts.

For bar charts, each bar (or vertical line) summarizes the data for one period of time. For example, each bar on a daily bar chart plots the open, high, low and closing prices for a single day (Figure 2.1).

Figure 2.1

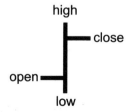

Example – sample OHLC values for S&P 500 Index

The table below shows the open, high, low and close values (often abbreviated to "OHLC") for the S&P 500 Index for four days in August 2007.

Date	Open	High	Low	Close
28-Aug-07	1,467	1,467	1,432	1,432
29-Aug-07	1,432	1,464	1,432	1,464
30-Aug-07	1,464	1,468	1,451	1,458
31-Aug-07	1,458	1,481	1,458	1,474

As can be seen, on 28 August the market opened at 1,467 (also the highest value of the day) and closed at 1,432 (also the low of the day). The following day, the reverse happened: the market opened at the low of the day and rose all day to close at the high of the day. On 30 August, the market opened at 1,464, climbed to the high of the day (1,468), then fell to the low of the day (1,451), and then finally partially recovered to close at 1,458. On a daily bar chart, the OHLC values for 30 August would be represented as shown in the following figure.

Figure 2.2

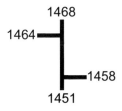

Over time, the bars for all the days rise and fall to form the trends and patterns chartists analyse.

Overlays on price action

Certain indicators can be drawn directly on price action and are used to show where prices are with regard to recent periods of time and how the price action itself is behaving. All of these overlays are derivatives of price.

Moving averages are what the name implies: mathematical averages of recent price action that are recalculated for each period. The result is a dynamic value that moves over time.

Chartists use moving averages to quantify the direction of price action. For example, if a short-term moving average is rising, or increasing in value over time, then in a short-term time frame there is a rally in progress. If prices themselves are above the average then the market is considered to be bullish, again, in that specific time frame.

A typical way to use averages is to buy when prices move above the average and sell when they move below. However, this is a very simplistic method and is best left for understanding the market rather than buying or selling anything.

Indicators beneath (or above) price action

Other indicators are plotted not as overlays in the main area of the chart but in their own portions of the chart.

> Before reading on, take this as a warning that some jargon and esoteric concepts are coming. Do not fret about them. This book will stick to the basics so treat this section as informational. There will not be a test at the end!

There are many types of indicators here, including non-price indicators, such as volume and sentiment readings, price derivative indicators, such as momentum, and more complex indicators that are based on price and volume, such as money flow.

Most of the indicators that are drawn here typically move from high values to low values and back. Contrast this to price action that can move for long periods of time in a trend and rest for long periods in patterns. Most indicators are confined to ranges of zero to 100 or −100 to +100 and look more like sine waves. Their positions within their respective ranges are what chartists watch.

Basic shapes and their meanings

Volumes of technical analysis textbooks have been written on the myriad of shapes and features seen on charts. We are only going to go into the most basic in the group and, fortunately, that will help us understand a huge percentage of all of them. Most are simply advanced forms of the others and we are only after the general meanings, not the demanding minutia.

Their differences can yield clues to what might happen but the basic concept for all of them is the same. Prices at the lower borders of the patterns look cheap and prices at the upper borders look expensive. Bulls and bears can hold their views on cheap and expensive, or one or both can change their views as the pattern progresses. For example, if the bulls start to get more aggressive at the bottom of the pattern, the lower border of the pattern itself will start to angle higher.

This can give us some idea of which way the market may emerge but, as we'll see later, we always must let the market tell us which way it wants to move by acting only after the market breaks free from the patterns. If the breakout is to the upside, then

> We always must let the market tell us which way it wants to move by acting only after the market breaks free from the patterns.

demand beat supply and we should buy. What was once thought to be expensive is now thought to be cheap. Conversely, if the break is to the downside, then supply beat demand and we should sell, as what was once thought to be cheap is now thought to be expensive.

As mentioned before, the market can only be in one of three phases: rising, falling or resting. Within the resting phase, the market can either be regrouping before continuing in the direction it was in, or changing in order to move in the opposite direction from which it was in. The shapes on the chart give us clues to which phase the market is in, whether that phase is ending and what might happen when it does end.

 But no matter how fancy the patterns get, our only job is to figure out what we are to do about it – buy, sell or hold. When we look at it that way, it is not so complicated.

There are many complex shapes to analyse but let's just keep with the basics. Each is named for its appearance (what it looks like on the chart) and can lean bullish or bearish depending on where it forms in a trend. This concept will become much clearer later so don't try to absorb it now.

The shapes are:

1. *rectangle* (also known as a *trading range*)

2. *triangle* (also known as a *pennant* or *wedge*)

3. *flag* (similar to the others but with a bit more directional forecasting ability)

4. *saucer* (or *rounded top/bottom*)

The differences may be subtle, or they may be extreme, but the bottom line is that the market is pausing and when it decides which way it wants to go from there, we just follow along.

What creates the chart?

All of the fancy pictures and indicators are what investors can see, but as with any structure it is the foundation that holds the whole thing up. For charts, that foundation is made from data. Buys and sells, how much was traded, and when those trades happened, all make up the data and with these data there is an added benefit over other types of data – reliability.

Unlike other methods where inputs are created by analysts (e.g. forward earnings) or government entities (e.g. housing starts), the data used in charting are fixed forever in time. There are no revisions, no restatements and no guesses. Whatever the market generated in terms of transaction price, share volume and investor sentiment, does not change later.

More importantly, analysis and investment strategies are more reliable. You cannot undo a stock purchase next month when the assumptions under which you bought it are revised. With

> Whatever the market generated in terms of transaction price, share volume and investor sentiment, does not change later.

charts, the assumptions never change. Your conclusions as a human being might change with the benefit of hindsight, but that cannot be blamed on the market. The market gave you data and that data will never change.

Stock splits

We must take a moment to mention stock splits and that they do not affect chart analysis. For example, if a stock splits two for one, an original investment of 100 shares now becomes 200 shares but at half the price. The value of your holdings is unchanged.

Charts will adjust for that split but the entire series of data adjusts. All historical prices are cut in half and all historical volumes are doubled. In that way, the value of shares traded each day, week or month remains exactly the same. The shape of the chart and all of its indicators looks exactly the same, too.

Everything supports price

For those with a marketing background, schools used a diagram resembling a table to describe the pieces of the marketing puzzle, with the product itself as the top surface. All other supporting functions, such as pricing, distribution channels and advertising, created the legs of the table. The more legs and the stronger they were, the more stable the table.

For the financial and commodity markets, the price of the stock or commodity is the top of the table (see Figure 2.3). Indicators such as momentum, sentiment, volume and anything else we can create, are the legs of the table. Everything is there to support the price and as long as we keep this in mind we will be properly focused on what we are doing. The stronger the "legs" the better the "table" (investment).

Figure 2.3

Price is the only thing that matters at the end of the day. It is what we say when someone asks where a stock is today and it is the only way we judge our investing success. Price rules and it is entirely possible to analyse a chart without any of the other supporting indicators. However, the others make our job a lot easier so let's learn the basics.

- **Price**

  The stuff you put in the bank. Clearly, this is the most important component as we measure our success in monetary terms. It only matters if we have more money after investing than when we started and that is measured by price.

- **Volume**

  How much money is moving. If price tells us what is going on, volume tells us how much is going on. Chart analysis depends on liquidity and crowd psychology, so the more shares of stock that are traded, the more reliable the analysis can be.

- **Momentum**

  How fast it got there. It is important to know how eager the crowd is to buy and sell because if it gets over enthused it will push prices out of equilibrium. Prices that move too far, too fast are prone to snapbacks.

- **Structure**

  The structure of the market refers to how it got to where it is now and we understand that by studying trends and patterns. As stocks trade, their ups and downs form patterns on the charts. Analysis of trends and patterns help us sort it all out and give us clear guidelines to know when a trend changes to a pattern or a pattern changes into a trend.

- **Sentiment**

  How people feel about the market. Contrarianism is based on the idea that the crowd gets it wrong when bull markets are changing to bear and vice versa. The masses seem to pile into the market just at the wrong time, but we must look at it in reverse. Just when everyone is buying, for example, is the wrong time to own stocks. Demand becomes exhausted and without demand, prices must stop going up, if not fall. So, when sentiment indicators reach extreme optimism or pessimism, the prevailing trend is likely to be nearing its end.

We must remember, however, that the crowd is right during the bulk of a trend. We must limit sentiment analysis to extreme readings only.

3. Understanding Each Part Of A Chart

Charts of stocks and indices are no more mysterious than charts of the weather or your family tree. Indeed, financial market charts may even be easier to understand since there is only one concept being charted – the performance of an investment over time.

If an experienced chart reader only had a single chart showing price vs. time, he or she would be quite able to determine many conditions of the stock or index including its trend, if that trend were changing and even if it would be a good idea or a bad idea to own it.

The process is not unlike a medical doctor observing a patient, noting symptoms and then diagnosing his or her condition. For most ailments, that would be sufficient. For more complex sets of symptoms, perhaps further tests would be needed. For complex financial situations, charting also has diagnostic tools for investors to use.

There are as many tools and indicators available as there are grains of sand at the beach, but the overwhelming majority of them fall into five categories:

1. Price
2. Volume
3. Momentum
4. Structure
5. Sentiment

The more of these categories used, the better the decision to buy or sell becomes.

Let's briefly review the basic concepts of the chart.

As mentioned, technical analysis is based on human behaviour. Investors and traders tend to react in similar ways in similar situations and this is the basis for the formation of trends and patterns on the charts. Therefore, if we can spot a "similar situation" on the chart today (e.g. a triangle pattern) then we can take action if and when that situation changes. Chartists call that a *breakout.*

We will now look in some detail at the five categories.

1. Price

Price action on a chart is the direct result of the buying and selling activities of investors, traders, institutions and governments. If a transaction is made, its price is recorded and a history of transaction prices creates the charts.

Price action tells us what the supply and demand equilibrium is at any given point in time. When prices move to form a trend, we know, in the case of a rising trend, that buyers are more aggressive than sellers. Eventually, equilibrium is restored and the market pauses.

Price is by far the most important aspect of charting for the simple reason that the difference between the price of a stock when it is bought and when it is sold is the ultimate determination of success for an investor. Profit is the only result of investment activity

> Price action tells us what the supply and demand equilibrium is at any given point in time.

that can be put in the bank and it does not matter that we based decisions on mathematically elegant models to get it.

Using price action

The trends and patterns formed by price action determine the structure of the market and are used to forecast future price movements. It is not a crystal ball but rather an assessment of probabilities.

We'll discuss this more in the *Structure* section later in this chapter.

2. Volume

If price tells the story about what is happening, volume tells the story about how much we can believe it. For example, if a stock rises one point on a volume of 50,000 shares, we can say that buyers dominated the day. But if the same stock rose one point on a volume of 500,000 shares, we can say that the gain had real significance. Enough people were interested enough to buy the stock that something must have changed.

We don't know what it was but it was important enough to get a lot people to take action. Perhaps it was earnings news or a lawsuit. From the charting point of view, the reason is less important as the actual event – the high volume gain in price.

Using volume

Volume is very useful in determining whether a stock is pulling back in a correction or changing direction. It also helps us determine whether it is forming a pattern or starting to move in earnest. For example, if a stock rallies 10 points and then pulls back ("corrects") two points, and volume on the pullback falls, it suggests that people were simply taking profits and not selling with any urgency. We can have confidence buying it when the trend resumes higher.

Another important use for volume is in the identification of both final panic (capitulation) and initial surges as investor moods change from one extreme to another. The former can be described as exhaustion, capitulation or a climax, when the last holdouts finally join the party en masse. Supply or demand, depending on which way prices are moving, is finally all used up and the trend ends.

For the latter, an initial surge, breakout or breakaway occurs when the public suddenly decides that a stock is cheap (or expensive) at the same time. It could be due to positive earnings news or it could be a situation when the time is just

> Volume is very useful in determining whether a stock is pulling back in a correction or changing direction.

right for investors to play "follow the leader" in buying. Whatever the reason, prices move sharply and volume surges.

Chart 3.1

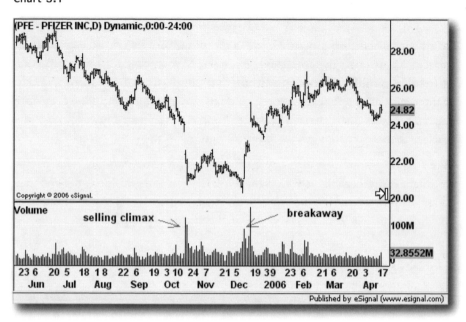

Here we see Pfizer with both a selling climax and a breakaway. In October 2005, the stock was already in a declining trend when it released a very poor earnings report on October 19. The stock spent the next two days in freefall as volume surged to well over 100 million shares per day. The last bulls had finally given up with a "get me out at any price" attitude and that marked the end of the declining trend. Supply was finally exhausted.

But just because the sellers have sold all they had, does not mean that there is an abundance of buyers ready to take the stock up again. Pfizer was mired in a low range for two months until a mid-December legal ruling went in the company's favour. The public finally believed the stock to be cheap and the sea change in attitude sent prices soaring on huge volume.

In both cases, volume tipped us off to changes in trend.

Astute readers will now ask why the second spike in volume was not a buying climax since prices were already moving higher. The answer is that the trend was only a few days old, unlike the declining trend leading into the October selling climax, which was months in the making. There just was not enough time nor profits earned to create a sentiment condition where the buyers have that "get me in at any price" attitude.

> The last bulls had finally given up with a "get me out at any price" attitude and that marked the end of the declining trend.

3. Momentum

Momentum indicators quantify what the naked eye can tell us about price action. Momentum in the markets is similar to momentum in physics in that a trend in motion tends to stay in motion unless an event occurs to stop it. Momentum in the market causes trends to stay in effect until halted by such outside forces as interest rates, earnings announcements, politics and anything else that changes investor perceptions of the stock's future.

This comes from human nature, as does almost everything else in the markets. If someone buys a stock and it goes up a little, his or her friend may want to buy it and it goes up a little more. Multiply this by thousands of investors, traders and institutions and the trickle of the stream becomes the immense force of a mighty river.

How many people were drawn into the bubble of 1999-2000 when they saw how much money their friends were making by trading? The lure of big profits feeds upon itself and we get a market driven by momentum. As long as the momentum is there, new money will come in.

Of course, it works on the way down, too. Fear spreads, maybe even faster than greed, and investors sell good stocks with the bad.

Using momentum

Momentum can also be moderate and such conditions are conducive for sustaining price trends. Chart watchers want to see strong momentum indicting a powerful yet controlled rally. Excessive momentum and an accelerating trend slope suggest that investors and traders are getting a bit too excited to buy and such a state does not result in a sustainable trend. In other words, it is a warning that the market is getting overheated.

The chart of DuPont shows three states of momentum of interest to chartists (see Chart 3.2). The first, in February 2005, shows a momentum indicator (relative strength index in this case, but do not worry about this for now) at an

> How many people were drawn into the bubble of 1999-2000 when they saw how much money their friends were making by trading?

extreme high level. The jargon for this condition is "overbought" but it really means that the trend began to move too far too fast. As a rubber band stretched too tightly, the market tends to snap back. It may not do that immediately but it does set up a high risk condition.

Chart 3.2

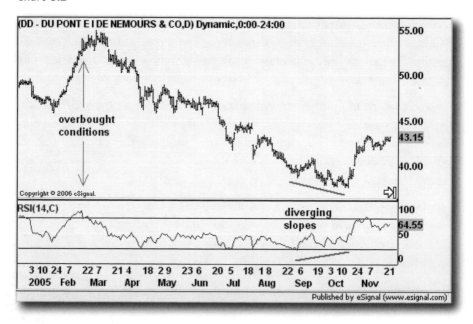

From June through August, momentum readings were showing strong downside movement and the trend lower continued. However, in September, momentum readings made higher lows while prices made lower lows. The stock was falling but each push lower had less power behind it. The bears were getting tired and the divergence between price action and indicator correctly foretold a change in direction.

4. Structure

The way price action is used on charts is two-fold. Either the stock in question is moving or it is not. The former creates a trend, either higher or lower. The latter creates resting zones and, further, the shapes of these resting zones give us clues as to when the next trend – up or down – may begin. It is the *structure* of these ups, downs and flats that is analysed.

Just as with an automobile heading out for a long journey, trending markets need to rest occasionally to refuel. This is where the bulls and the bears are taking their profits, licking their wounds and rethinking their strategies.

The chart of E-Trade in 2005, shows two trading ranges or pauses within trends that served as resting phases for the stock (see Chart 3.3). The first range earlier in the year had a classic shape and gave a clear signal when the declining trend resumed. If any investors thought the stock was cheap at that time, the breakdown told them that they were wrong and to look elsewhere for an investment.

Chart 3.3

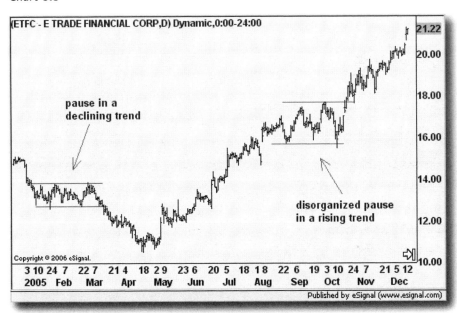

Later in the year, there was another resting phase but this time it was a bit more irregular. The chart itself may not have given the novice chart reader confidence to buy on its own, but it definitely confirmed the positive fundamental news that was released at that time.

The next chart, DuPont again, shows a trading range acting as a transition from one trend to another (see Chart 3.4).

Chart 3.4

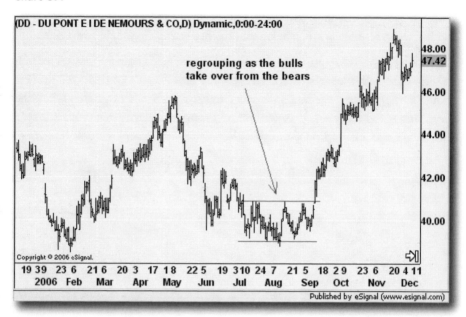

This time, prices move out from the range in the opposite direction from the trend that was in force and a new trend begins.

Definition of trend

The textbooks say that:

- a *rising trend* is a series of prices that make ever-increasing highs and lows over time. Conversely,

- a *falling* or *declining trend* is a series of prices that make ever-decreasing highs and lows over time.

Both can occur in any time frame, from intraday to annually or longer, and both can exist at the same time. For example, a price pullback in a bull market is simply a short-term falling trend in a longer-term rising trend.

Despite the wiggles on the chart and a two-month period of rising prices in the summer of 2006, the overriding trend for Advanced Micro Devices (AMD) was down (see Chart 3.5). Some may think that the stock was cheap in January 2007 – but was it? No matter what the fundamentals might say, the market is telling us that supply is still overwhelming demand and forcing prices lower.

Chart 3.5

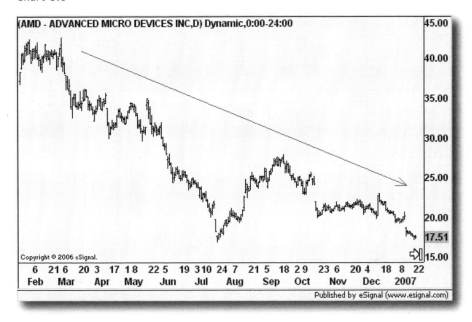

Chart 3.6 shows the same stock three months later, with the arrow on the chart in the same position it was in Chart 3.5.

Chart 3.6

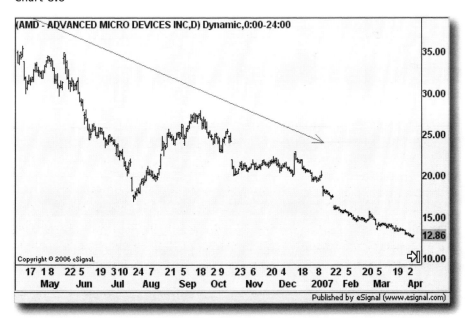

The price dropped from 17.51 to 12.86 – a staggering 26% loss on a stock that already looked cheap on the surface. Keep in mind that there was a bull market going on in the stock market at the time with a temporary, albeit significant dip, in February. The trend in AMD was down, so no matter what justifications were made for buying the stock, the market disagreed. And the market is the boss.

> The trend in AMD was down, so no matter what justifications were made for buying the stock, the market disagreed. And the market is the boss.

What do trends form?

As mentioned, there are only three states in which a stock can be – rising, falling or staying the same. Of course, there are different degrees of each but since there are only three courses of action investors can take – buy, sell or hold – how fast a stock is rising is irrelevant. We cannot "sort of" buy it. Either we buy it or we don't.

> We cannot "sort of" buy it. Either we buy it or we don't.

Granted, a stock in a strong bull market would likely inspire us to buy more shares than if it were barely moving at all. The strength of the bull market determines how much we buy but not whether we buy it at all.

> A trend is also just another term for bull or bear markets of varying degrees.

The chart of Transocean from 2003-2006, shows a bullish trend (see Chart 3.7). There were small pullbacks along the way, but for an investor considering a purchase of this stock in 2006, despite prices that had more than tripled in just a few years, the trend was up and therefore any decision to hold on or even buy more on the next pullback based on fundamental analysis or a broker's recommendation would get the market's blessing.

Chart 3.7

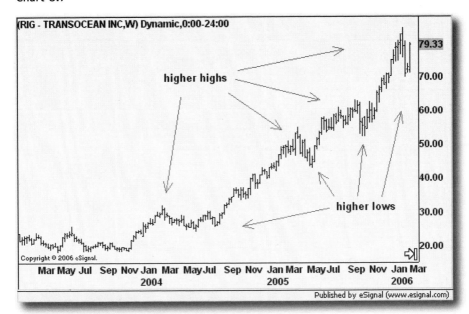

Clearly, this stock is a case of buying high and hoping to sell even higher. The stock went on to touch the 90 level within two weeks before experiencing its first major pullback (see Chart 3.8). But even when things were looking bleak for investors in mid-2006, Transocean never traded below its previous significant low and went on to reach 109 a year later. That is not a bad return, even for an investment made just before the 2006 correction set in.

Chart 3.8

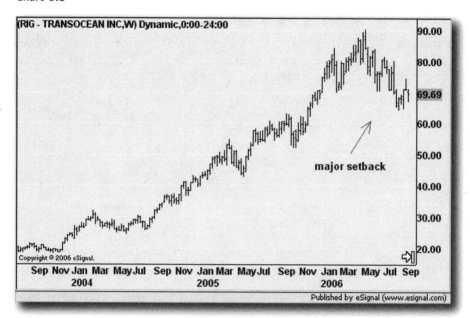

Trends exist because information flow around the market is imperfect. If everyone knew at the same time and in the same manner that company X just secured a new contract for business, then its stock would jump from where it was trading to a new price level immediately. There would be no gradual change in price and no bull market. It would be trading here today and tomorrow it would be trading there, where prices would remain until the next change in fundamentals occurs.

However, people do not get their information at the same rate and they do not assimilate it in the same manner. They also do not have the same investment time frames. In short, they do not have the same perceptions, at least not all at the same time, and this is why a stock gradually moves from one price level to another.

What are support and resistance?

The following paragraph has been covered before, but is offered here to keep the flow of this chapter smooth.

If a stock is trending higher, it will eventually encounter price levels at which it finds resistance to its advance. Resistance is also another name for supply because at that level, investors collectively decide that value has been reached and they sell their shares. Supply increases and demand may also decrease.

Depending on how aggressive buyers and sellers are, the price of the stock will either pause or decline.

The converse is true at support. At some price level, a falling stock price will stabilize. Enough investors will perceive it to be good value and demand shares while others will perceive the price to be too low for them to want to sell any more of their holdings.

If:

- at *resistance*: demand for shares increases enough to absorb all the supply being offered for sale then prices stop moving. However, if demand overwhelms supply then prices must rise and the stock breaks free from resistance. **Chartists will take that as a buy signal.**

- at *support*: if investors continue to supply shares and demand cannot absorb it all then prices will break down. **Chartists will take that as a sell signal.**

In Chart 3.9, Dell Computers encountered resistance several times in 2001 and 2002. Investors decided as a group that shares were expensive so they sold, increasing supply and sending prices lower.

Chart 3.9

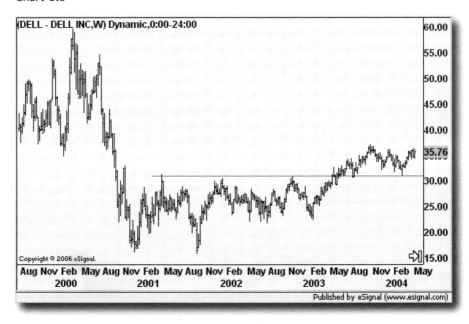

In 2003, the stock moved above resistance (a *breakout*) as investor perception changed from that price being expensive to being cheap.

Resistance becomes support

It is very common for resistance to flip to support and vice versa. After the market decides that the breakout price is now cheap, any pullback to that level will draw in buyers who missed their first opportunity to buy. They demand shares and that price level becomes support.

This action happens far into the future, too, as the market has memory, even if individual investors do not. A 20-year-old investor is not going to have experience with a major price bottom that happened 25 years ago, but the market will. Remember, the market is the sum of all investors and analysts within, so historical charts will show major turning points from the past that still have significance today.

> The market has memory, even if individual investors do not.

What is a chart pattern?

When support and resistance levels occur near to one another, patterns begin to take shape. The simplest of these is a trading range where prices move from a lower level to a higher level and back again, as illustrated on the chart of Yahoo from 2001-2003 (see Chart 3.10).

Chart 3.10

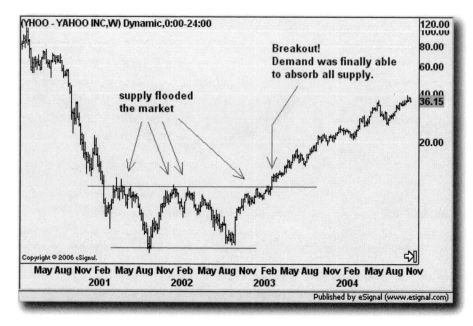

The trading range followed the bear market of 2000-2001, and represented a healing period for the stock. At the bottom of the range, investors found the stock to be cheap and demand picked up enough to send prices higher. At the top of the range, it was the opposite – investors found the stock to be expensive and supply picked up enough to send prices lower.

However, in early 2003, something changed investor perceptions of value and what was formerly viewed as expensive was now viewed as cheap. Demand was able to absorb all supply and prices finally were able to move higher.

All chart patterns are derivatives of this basic trading range.

Some have steady support levels but falling resistance levels over time. Others show support and resistance levels converging, forming a pennant shape. But no matter what the shape, all patterns are the same in that the stock is moving sideways rather than trending higher or lower, and breakouts above or below these patterns tell us that either demand or supply, respectively, has taken control.

The bottom line is that patterns and trends on charts yield clues as to the relationship between bulls and bears and when that relationship changes. We do not have to know why it changed other than it did change, and when we can identify it we can take appropriate action – either buy, sell or hold.

Patterns, patterns, patterns

There are many types of patterns on the charts and most have names that are rather obvious. A triangle pattern looks like a triangle. A flag pattern looks like a flag flying on a flagpole. However, despite many variations, and sometimes clever names, patterns fall into only the two categories discussed earlier: those that allow the stock to rest before continuing its trend higher or lower, and those that create a change in trend from up to down or from down to up.

Here are a few examples of the most common varieties.

Rectangles

We've already discussed rectangle patterns and called them trading ranges. It's all just a matter of semantics because both are patterns that contain the up and down wiggles of a sideways moving market.

Anadarko Petroleum formed a rectangle pattern in the summer of 2005 following a two-month rally (see Chart 3.11). After bouncing between support (the pattern bottom) and resistance (the pattern top) for two months, prices finally broke out to the upside and the trend continued higher.

Chart 3.11

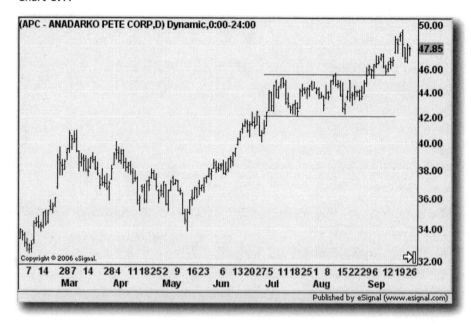

It is important to let the market prove that the rectangle is a pausing pattern within a rally by letting prices actually break out. Rectangles, and the other patterns described below, *usually* hint at the direction prices will move – with the original trend or in a new direction – but not all of the time. Waiting to see what actually happens allows the market to tell us what it is going to do rather than relying on us to make an educated guess.

Triangles

This type of continuation pattern has converging lines of support and resistance. Many analysts refer to triangles as "coils" because the trading action gets tighter and tighter, storing energy until the market breaks out with great force. The breakout usually, but not always, occurs in the direction of the original trend.

Chart 3.12

A long-term chart of Google shows a very clear series of rising bottoms and falling tops to create a triangle shape (see Chart 3.12). Each swing higher and lower within the pattern is marked with increased uncertainly as both bulls and bears lose conviction. Bulls are taking short-term profits sooner and sooner on each rally and, conversely, bears are covering their short positions sooner on each decline. The market is waiting for something to unleash the energy building in this coiling action and in September 2006, Google finally got that spark. The rally from the breakout point was swift.

Triangles come in several varieties. Google's triangle had a symmetrical shape and is labelled with that name – a *symmetrical triangle*. But there are other shapes, such as an *ascending triangle* where the bottom border rises and the top border is flat (See Chart 3.13).

Chart 3.13

ascending triangle

Hanover Compressor sported an ascending triangle in early 2007, before breaking out to the upside. Don't let the empty space on the chart seen in February detract from the pattern. The rally at that point was just very steep, with some of it occurring between trading days, but the bottom line here is that Hanover formed an ascending triangle. When demand overwhelmed supply, prices moved higher from the pattern.

A descending triangle sports a falling upper border and a flat bottom. Theoretically, the bulls are not quite as eager to start buying the stock at short-term lows as the bears are to sell short-term highs. This suggests an eventual downside breakout but as always, we must wait for the market to actually break down before taking action.

Conversely, a descending triangle has a relatively flat bottom boundary and a falling top boundary. Kimco Realty shows two descending triangles in 2005, with the first breaking out to the upside and the second breaking down (see Chart 3.14). This is a good lesson that waiting for the market to make its move before taking any action is the best strategy.

Chart 3.14

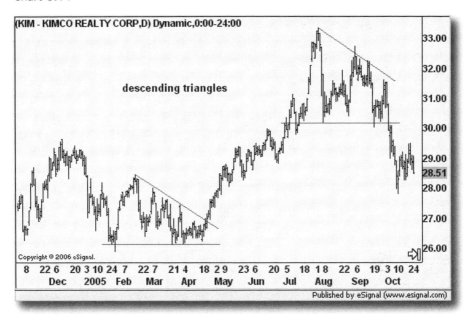

Another important point to keep in mind when analysing triangles is that a breakout is significant if it occurs approximately two thirds to three quarters of the way from the left side of the triangle to the apex (the apex is where the two lines would meet if they were extended). If the price action continues to bounce around in the triangle close to the apex, a breakout needs to be significant in terms of the power of the move. Kimco's early 2005 triangle exhibited a steep price move, so it could be believed.

Flags

The most common of the continuation patterns is called a flag because it resembles a flag flying on a flagpole. When a market is trending higher, it is more common for it to slowly give back some of those gains as the bulls take some profits. Since traders do not all do this at the same time, the market displays a small counter trend lower as more of them take their profits. When this is over, the market generally breaks out in the direction of the original trend as the bulls take over again.

Chart 3.15

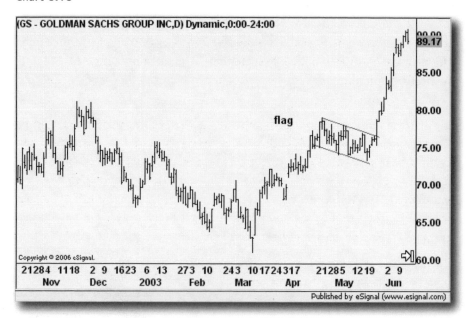

Goldman Sachs was participating in the broad market rally that began in March 2003 (see Chart 3.15). In late April, it settled into a corrective decline that was relatively shallow and orderly. Lower highs and lower lows formed the pattern and when prices moved above the upper border, the rally resumed. The correction was over.

More patterns

There are as many varieties of chart pattern as there are chartists. But each is a variation on the theme that the market is resting, either to continue its current journey or to change direction and head the other way.

The reader will encounter *head-and-shoulders*, *saucers*, *gaps*, *islands*, and even the *Prussian Helmut*, but don't let the names and strange shapes worry you. Everything you need is covered in this book. The ability to recognize the others just makes you that much better.

5. Sentiment

Jargon alert! Sentiment analysis is the least understood aspect of charting. The data are unusual and include such items as polls of investor attitudes and the implied volatility of index options – items that are often foreign concepts to most investors.

It is also the most counterintuitive of analyses as it signals a bearish condition when it reaches its most bullish levels. Conversely, it is bullish when it reaches its most bearish levels. For example, if a survey of investors reveals 75% to be bullish, expecting the market to be higher in three months, 15% to be neutral and 10% to be bearish, and if the normal amount of bulls is 40% and bears 30%, then we can see how the overall posture of investors has shifted to a very bullish level. If everyone is bullish, then who is left to buy?

Put another way, from where is the demand going to come? Sooner or later, something triggers a change in attitude and there is a rush to sell stocks. Prices

> If everyone is bullish, then who is left to buy?

fall quickly as supply surges with little available demand to absorb it.

This is exactly the condition found at the end of major bear (or bull) markets when they transition into major bull (or bear) markets.

Because there are so many indicators available to clever data hounds, it is impossible to cover them all. Fortunately, usage for all of them is similar so let's just understand what is going on with investors' attitudes and we'll have 80% of what we need.

Life cycle of market attitudes

Sentiment is the summation of all market expectations. It ranges from fear and hopelessness to indifference to greed and complacency. At the bottom of a bear market, the expectations of market participants are almost unanimous for lower prices and more financial losses. But as Baron Rothschild said many decades ago, the best time to buy is when there is "blood in the streets". What that means is when nobody wants to talk about stocks – let alone buy them – it is the best time to become a bull.

This is called contrarian thinking – going against the crowd. Just be careful not to go against the crowd when sentiment is not at an extreme. Just because you disagree with something does not make you a contrarian.

As a rally begins, some of these participants become hopeful and prices rise off their worst levels. In the middle of the bull market, many investors have changed their expectations, but not everyone is bullish. There are still some doubters left to provide demand when they finally decide to join in.

Near the end of the rally, almost everyone is assuming that the trend will continue. More risks are taken and greed becomes dominant. In other words, market sentiment is at an extreme high. When everyone is euphoric about stocks and office water cooler talk turns to trading from more traditional pop culture topics, it is the best time to start selling stocks.

> When nobody wants to talk about stocks – let alone buy them – it is the best time to become a bull.

Pulling it all together

Critics will point out that forecasting future price movement based on past price movement is akin to reading a crystal ball or divining the future from the textures of chicken entrails. The most vocal practitioners of fundamental analysis are quick to call technical analysis financial voodoo. It sounds like they are defending their turf rather than keeping their minds open!

Indeed, chart watchers cannot predict the future any better than your broker, your spouse or a Ouija board. But what they can do better than most is make a decision about what to do – buy, sell or hold – based on the probabilities of the actions of others given certain conditions. In other words, if a pattern on the chart appears, a chart watcher can create a framework for what the market might do if and when prices break free from that pattern. It does not work every time, but past performance does give us an idea of what will happen so we can do something about it.

For example, if a stock is rising and then starts to move sideways as bulls and bears become uncertain as to what to do next, a coiling pattern appears on the chart as price swings in both directions diminish (a triangle pattern – refer back to Chart 3.12).

Typically, when such a pattern appears after a reasonable trend it represents a resting period. Chart watchers wait for prices to move above the upper border of the triangle and then buy the stock because the odds favour further gains.

Why?

Because such an event represents a shift in the market, where a price range that was once considered to be expensive is suddenly considered to be cheap. We do not have to concern ourselves with what happened to cause that change in opinion specifically, but only that it did happen.

But even with such a breakout from the pattern, chart watchers do not know for sure that the stock will go up, and they do not know how long it might take. What they do know is that the probability of making money by owning the stock is good.

The cruel yet kind master

Since chart watching is not infallible, an even more important aspect is that it will tell us quickly if our assessment of the market's mood is incorrect.

For example, if prices move higher from the triangle pattern in the chart and then fall back within that pattern, we will know that we were incorrect in our original decision to buy. Either we missed something on the chart or the market simply changed its mind and decided to go down. We sell immediately and book our small loss, leaving our egos at the door.

Something chart watchers keep pasted to their computer screens is a sticky note that says:

All big losses begin as small losses

When the initial reason for buying is gone, we don't hang around hoping it will go back up. Hope is a four-letter word in the world of investing.

If a chart watcher follows breakouts, he or she will inevitably have losing trades. But if he or she is disciplined and responds to breakout failures, the losses will be small and easily overwhelmed by the profits from winning trades. In this regard, charts help manage risk.

Sometimes there just isn't any pattern at all

There are times when technical analysis will not be able to decipher the market's message. Perhaps a pattern is too irregular or too vague. Certainly, analysis of a stock with low trading volume or a very thin float (shares outstanding) cannot be as reliable because, by definition, technical analysis seeks to measure the psychology of the crowd, and that demands liquidity.

Chart 3.16

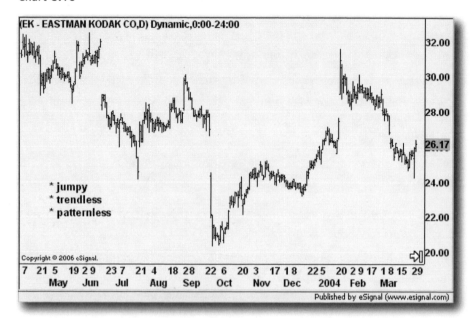

Sometimes there is nothing useful on the chart. Despite a multitude of indicators, patterns and trends must jump off the chart because anything else required the user to force his or her own opinions on what is

> Sometimes a barking dog is just barking and not saying anything.

happening (see Chart 3.16). Sometimes a barking dog is just barking and not saying anything.

If you don't see anything, it's not there. It is an important point to remember.

Further, a stock embroiled in legal battles, takeover activity or geopolitical problems is going to be rocked by news events and not by normal market forces. There is no shame in avoiding these securities simply because market forces are taking a back seat to other forces.

4. How To Use Charts – The Basics

In order to have a plan we need to set some goals. Obviously, making money is the main goal, but that is far too broad a goal to use to set up specific actions to take. Let's keep it as simple as possible and just use charts to complement what you are already doing with other investment methods.

Sanity check

Even if investors use other forms of market analysis to find stocks to buy and sell, technical analysis can easily exist in a supporting role. Knowing what the market itself thinks about your investment candidates can confirm the stronger ones and keep you from bad risks with the weaker ones. In other words, it can help determine if the market agrees or disagrees.

Is the trend up?

Stocks can have low prices but not be cheap. Clearly, there will be times when a stock has been shunned for so long despite improving fundamentals that it presents good value for investors. However, there are also times when a stock is down in price for a reason and will be likely to continue to go down for quite a while longer. The trend can help us differentiate between a value play and a dying stock.

Conversely, stocks can have high prices but not be expensive. The chart of Taser International is a case in point (see Chart 4.1). This stock was a penny stock (trading at less than one dollar) in March 2003, but in less than one year was trading at 11! Certainly, that would have been a great excuse to take profits, and indeed a major Wall Street brokerage firm issued a sell rating only a few days earlier.

Chart 4.1

But three months later, the stock was trading at 30 for a tripling in price on top of the 30-fold increase seen the year before (see Chart 4.2). The trend was up! It was steep but it was still rising.

Chart 4.2

Jargon alert! Note that these charts are drawn using *semi-logarithmic scaling,* which is a method of plotting price changes as percentages rather than absolute values. A constant rate of increase means that the percentage of price gains was constant even though the absolute changes increased over time. Chartists use this type of scaling when dealing with very large percentage price ranges or very long spans of time (measured in years).

If you liked it here, then...

Let's say a stock or even a sector in the market held several buy ratings by analysts and its price moves down a bit. Nothing changed at the company and there was no bad news, yet prices were down.

A bargain, right?

Maybe.

The widely followed Philadelphia Stock Exchange semiconductor index was enjoying a multi-month rally into the new year 2004 (see Chart 4.3). As January yielded to February, this solid sector looked to be a better deal – a sale price for the same merchandise, so to speak.

Chart 4.3

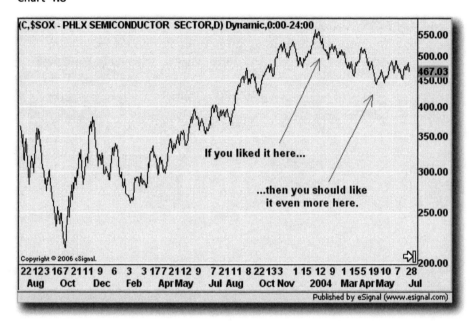

(C,$SOX - PHLX SEMICONDUCTOR SECTOR,D) Dynamic,0:00-24:00

If you liked it here...

...then you should like it even more here.

But by March it became apparent that the index was no longer in a rising trend. By April, it had lost roughly 18%, so if you liked it before, at this price you should like it even more, right? It is a trap into which investors can fall very easily because one look at the chart with the naked eye reveals that the market tone had changed. The trend was down.

Chart 4.4

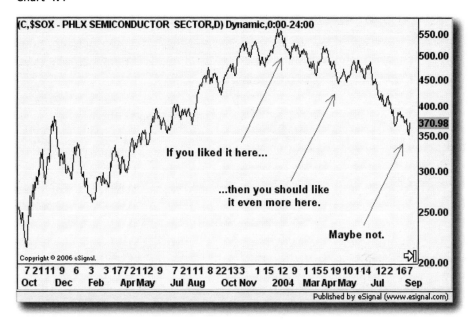

(C,$SOX - PHLX SEMICONDUCTOR SECTOR,D) Dynamic,0:00-24:00

If you liked it here...

...then you should like
it even more here.

Maybe not.

Copyright © 2006 eSignal.

Published by eSignal (www.esignal.com)

If we thought it was a good value in April, after an 18% discount, we were dead wrong. By September, the index was down by twice that percentage (see Chart 4.4). The trend said it all.

We've established that the trend had changed from up to down but how do we quantify it?

In other words, where do we draw a trendline that will be useful for making buy or sell decisions in the near future? A clear trendline was drawn in the previous chart, connecting the tops of interim price swings just as the textbook says it should be done, but prices are quite far away from that line. The trendline is no longer as useful as it was when prices were closer.

We cannot really define what "close" is, but a good rule of thumb is to see how far away prices moved from the trendline in the past. In this case, we can see that they are much farther away than before and that means looking for help in other indicators.

Finally cheap

The next chart shows a simple momentum indicator with a very strange name – *MACD* (moving average convergence divergence) – but almost any similar indicator will do (see Chart 4.5). Remember, an indicator is just a derivative of price in the same manner that acceleration is a derivative of velocity in the world of physics. It measures how fast a stock or index's trend is changing.

Chart 4.5

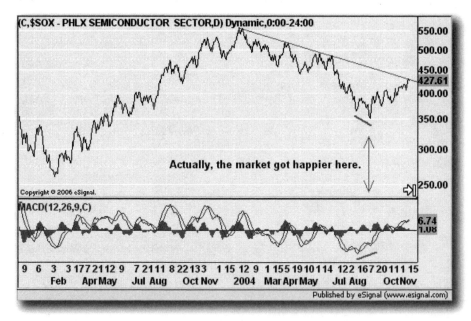

The indicator made a higher low while prices made a lower low. It is a classic sign that downside momentum was waning and a good place to look for a rally to begin. Finally, the market was saying that the stock – or index, in this case – was cheap.

A bad reaction to good news

It's not the news that matters to a chart watcher but rather how a stock reacts to it. While stocks usually move higher when good news happens, often they move in the opposite direction, and that is where there is information for chartists. The market is telling them that something is wrong.

For a bad reaction to good news, it's not that the news was false but rather that investors had pushed up the stock's price in advance of the news release. Somebody usually knows something or thinks he or she knows

> It's not the news that matters to a chart watcher but rather how a stock reacts to it.

something, beforehand (not illegally). They begin to buy, adding to demand, and the stock can rally.

Then the news comes out and only perfection would be good enough to draw more buyers in. The stock falls and the old saw:

buy on rumour, sell on news

rings true once more.

One extreme example occurred during the stock market bubble that ended in 2000 (see Chart 4.6). Copper Mountain rallied back after the initial market sell off, and a few days before it was due to release its quarterly earnings the stock surged more than 25%. The day earnings came out the stock collapsed and never saw that price level again. Investors should have run away from this stock, taking losses if necessary, because the worst was yet to come.

Chart 4.6

As an aside, several months later, when prices were down approximately 65% from the peak, an analyst issued a buy rating. After all, with that kind of price decline, certainly it was a good risk, if not a good value. But the trend was down and the stock continued its death march into bankruptcy. Say it again: *the trend was down.*

Value play or dying stock?

There are many reasons why a stock price moves higher or lower. The environment for stocks in general may be changing. The company's business is doing well or is not doing well, respectively. Perhaps the perception of a competitor's prospects is respectively sweetening or souring investor attitudes on the whole sector. Whatever the reason, people are buying and selling and the chart shows a trend.

The questions are:

- for a *bearish trend*: whether this lower level of pricing reflects a bargain or a warning that the worst is yet to come – as it did for Copper Mountain above.

- for a *bullish trend*: is the higher level of pricing reflecting good times ahead or simply an expensive stock?

Is the trend long in the tooth?

Trees don't grow to the clouds and bull markets don't last forever. Sooner or later, prices in the markets will – not can – but will decline. Fortunately, the market gives clues as to whether it has more life left in it or is ready to change course.

One extreme case with which many investors may be familiar is the sales call from a stockbroker hyping a new company that is the next Microsoft or Google. That company just may be what is promised, but more often than not the pitch includes such phrases as:

> *This bull market is going to last for years.*

> *Take advantage of the best market conditions we've seen in years.*

Or, the most dangerous:

> *Returns are projected to be X over the next ten years.*

Nobody can forecast returns a decade from now for a start-up company. All of these phrases assume that the world is different now, that the rules of the investment game have changed and that trends today can be

What the broker is doing is buying into the hype of an overheated market and passing it on to you.

extrapolated far into the future. But the market is too complex and non-linear to do any of that. What the broker is doing is buying into the hype of an overheated market and passing it on to you.

The fear and greed pendulum has swung all the way to greed. Which way will the pendulum move now? That's right, back to historical norms, if not swing all the way to fear.

Are there any warnings to heed?

Charts provide many early warning signals to help investors decide if it is time to take some profits. It also gives signals to keep investors out of the market in the first place when the odds of success are low. Entire books can be written on the subject of "when to sell" but we'll keep it simple, as promised, and cover just the basics. As with most parts of technical analysis, understanding the basics gives investors enough tools to be successful.

Waning momentum

When a ball is thrown up in the air, gravity slows its rate of ascent. Momentum starts to decline yet the ball continues higher, but at some point gravity equals the energy applied to the ball (the throw) and the ball momentarily stops. Finally, gravity takes over and the ball falls back to Earth.

In financial and commodity markets, the same concept applies. Investors as a group buy stocks, for example, until the number of new investors starts to decline. This means demand from buyers has slowed a bit but the stock can still advance with less power. But sooner or later, the momentum of the market stalls, allowing the sellers (supply) to take over.

The charts show this in advance, as can be seen in the early 2004 trend of the Dow Jones Real Estate Investment Trust (REIT) index (see Chart 4.7).

Chart 4.7

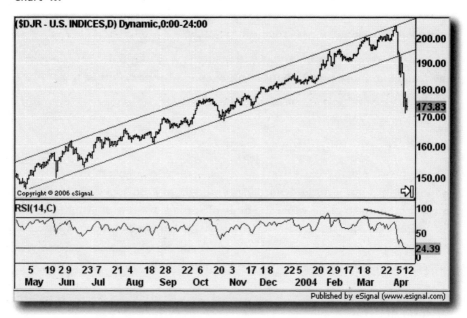

($DJR - U.S. INDICES,D) Dynamic,0:00-24:00

When price action and a momentum indicator diverge in direction, typically price action will change to the direction of the indicator. This REIT index example is a bit extreme in that we cannot predict such a swift decline, but that is not what this is all about. In March 2004, we got a good indication that we should not be buying REIT issues at that time. All we can control is our decision to buy, sell or hold, as clearly the charts were saying – at a minimum – *do not buy more*!

As a surgeon might say:

> *First, do no harm.*

In investing, sometimes the best investment is the one you do not make.

Declining demand (volume)

In a similar manner to waning momentum, waning volume is also a warning sign. Rising trends need broad and somewhat rising participation from the public so when volume starts to wane, so, too, does demand. Either the numbers of new buyers

> In investing, sometimes the best investment is the one you do not make.

has dwindled or something has happened to stop existing buyers from buying more. It does not matter which. The charts shows a divergence between price action and volume, giving us warning that something is not quite right.

Chart 4.8

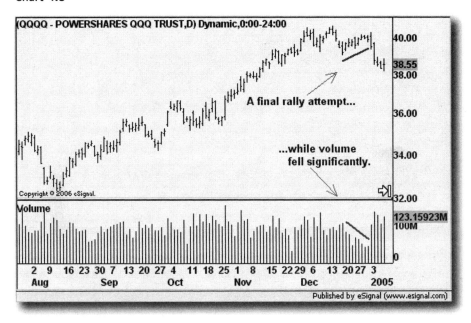

In late 2005, the Nasdaq-100 tracking ETF attempted to rally back to previous highs, but volume dried up significantly. While we have to take this with a pinch of salt due to this occurring during the year-end holidays, the implications of waning demand as prices rose was telling. On the first day of the new year, prices broke down and volume surged. Investors got a sign not to look for holiday bargains.

Supply waiting to come into the market

Investors have many reasons to sell their stocks and provide supply to the market. One of the easiest to spot is a resistance level – a price at which supply flooded the market in the past. Investors viewed that price as expensive before and unless something changes, such as corporate news, interest rates, overall market trend, etc., this price will cause at least some investors to sell.

Chart 4.9

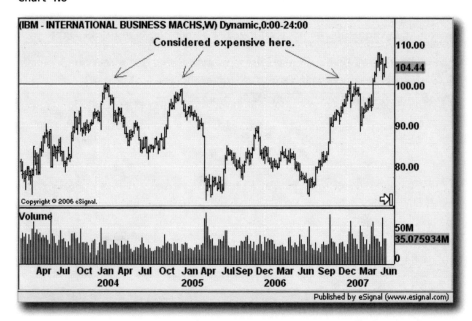

IBM could not break the 100 barrier for several years as investors considered it to be expensive there and sold (see Chart 4.9). Investors would have been well served to look at this resistance level and realize that the market was entering a zone where supply was waiting to come in. Purchases there would not have been advised.

But these levels do not last forever and when something changes in investor attitudes, stocks can break through these levels. In early 2007, the market was rebounding from a corrective dip and technology shares in particular were in favour again. IBM suddenly broke out from a short-term range and that turned sellers into buyers at the 100 level. It was a technical breakout.

Is there anyone left to buy?

Here are a few situations in question and answer format that play to investor sentiment. Again, if everyone is excited to own stocks, it is probably not a good time to buy them. Conversely, if everyone is jaded about stocks, or a type of stock, it is probably time to give them a new look.

Q: What does it mean when the neighbourhood tavern has CNBC (business channel) on the television and not ESPN (sports channel)?

A: The market is not at a bottom.

Q: What does it mean when the guys in the weekend football game are talking about how much money they are making trading?

A: The market is not at a bottom.

Q: What does it mean when the banks are offering new interest only and sub–prime mortgages?

A: The real estate market is not at a bottom.

Q: What does it mean when there are whole aisles in the supermarket dedicated to the Atkins (low carbohydrate) diet?

A: Time to buy bread and cereal stocks.

Q: What does it mean when *Time* magazine puts a picture of a bear on its cover, talking about how stocks are bad investments?

A: Time to look for a bottom in the market.

Q: What does it mean when *The Economist* magazine runs a cover story about how the world is awash with crude oil?

A: Time to buy energy stocks.

Q: What does it mean when *Business Week* runs a cover story about the new world of low interest rates?

A: Time to lock in a fixed rate mortgage.

These may be somewhat whimsical in presentation but the meanings should be clear. When the crowd is completely enamoured or disgusted with any particular investment, it is time to be a contrarian and go the other way.

Determine aggressiveness

If we are less sure about something, there is no law that says we have to go full force into it. There is no harm in prudent speculating with small amounts of money and proper risk management. Charts may present a good situation but not necessarily a great one. Or, they may present a good stock in a market that looks rather weak.

The point is that charts can also help investors know when to buy a lot or just a little.

Checking out an idea

Let's say your friend gave you a tip: buy Cameco Corp. It's September 2004, and he says that uranium is going to be the next market to soar. He shows you studies and he shows you fundamental valuations from the few analysts covering it. Not bad, you say, but you've been hurt before following tips.

So where is the news about this market? Nuclear power plants are still pariahs in the country and, apart from that, there is no other use for this commodity.

You go to the charts and you see that Cameco has already tripled over the past two years, but sure enough there is a bull market trend there (see Chart 4.10). Further, the stock had a decent sized correction in 2003, and since it has bounced back, you think that somebody has to be buying it. And look at the volume that has become the norm. Somebody is definitely buying it.

Chart 4.10

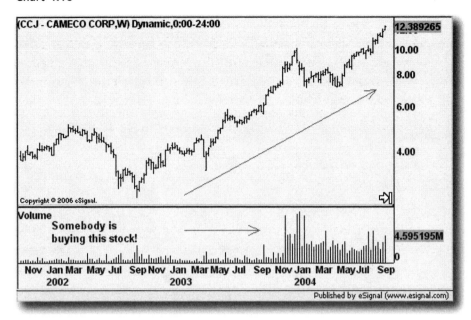

The recent breakout from the one-year range to new all-time highs, convinces you that there is more to come and you throw a little money at it. The chart – at a minimum – issued no negative warnings and more likely gave you the green light.

Long story short: the stock hit 16 within a year on its way to 55 by mid 2007. The charts did not demand that the stock be bought but they allowed you to act on a hot tip with the wind at your back.

Weighing your options – Should you invest at all?

Charts can even show the relative performance between different asset classes. A long-term chart of the ratio of 10-year Treasury notes to the Standard & Poor's 500 shows the periods of time favouring one asset over the other and how they shift (see Chart 4.11).

Chart 4.11

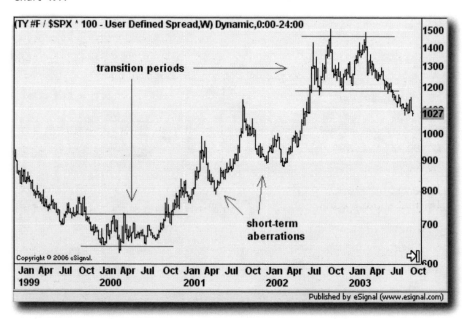

As the stock market was peaking in 2000, the performance ratio between notes and stocks was moving sideways in a churning pattern. When the ratio moved out from the pattern, the long period of stock market outperformance had completed its transition to underperformance. Clearly, it was time to emphasize bonds in a portfolio.

Conversely, in 2002 and 2003, the relationship stalled again to form a range and when it broke down we knew it was time to favour stocks again. Neither allowed us to catch the ultimate top or bottom, but knowing about this chart allowed us to get aggressive or more cautious when warranted.

There are short-term periods where the ratio appeared to be reversing course, but asset allocation is usually a longer-term process. In this example, ranges that lasted for months were good signs of transition and wiggles that lasted for weeks, or just a few months, were simply corrections.

How will this make you a better investor?

Let's say you have analyst reports that the stock of a company is undervalued based on earnings projections, new business pipelines and a deal made to acquire a small competitor in a key niche. You bring it to your investment club where you discuss its pros and cons, and as a group you overwhelmingly vote to buy some shares. In your account it goes and you sit back and wait for a nice profit to develop over time.

This is a typical way investors select stocks. Yet there is still something missing from the analysis. Nowhere have you considered whether the market thinks the stock is going to go up in price. Nowhere have the simple economic concepts of supply and demand for shares been factored in.

Why is that important?

The reason is that no matter what we human beings think about the valuation of a company, its stock is not going to go up in price unless there is greater demand for its shares by buyers than there is supply of shares by sellers. This is the core of chart analysis and it can confirm or deny what you have already learned about a company.

How one view can give you confidence in an investment

Here is an example of how a chart can confirm what fundamental, quantitative and economic analysis may have said was a good stock to buy. Keep in mind that we are only using prices without any indicators, so this should hammer home the point that charts are easy to use and provide a huge amount of information at their simplest level.

On May 17, 2005, a major Wall Street firm issued a buy recommendation on Cabot Oil & Gas (see Chart 4.12). Over the previous two months, the stock had been in a near free fall, so there had to be some worry that there was something wrong with the stock, despite the fundamental view that it was cheap.

Chart 4.12

The chart shows that prices landed on a support level – a price in the past at which investors started to aggressively buy this stock. Once again, demand could be expected to swell at this price and in this case, on the day the upgrade was issued, the stock did indeed jump up in price.

So should an investor join in with the professionals that trade when a favourite analyst makes a recommendation?

In this case, the market bounced off support to prove that demand increased, and that is a good sign that the market agreed with the analyst. Investors could have bought with increased confidence, and in this case it paid off quickly. Cabot reached a price of 26 by October of that year, nearly doubling the initial investment.

When charts agree with the fundamentals, the combination can be powerful.

But there is another reason investors could have been confident. The support level is also a *stop loss* level – the price below which the market is telling us that we were wrong. We risk a small amount, from purchase price to stop loss price, with the potential of making several times that in profits.

Why would we choose to cut our losses just below support?

Any market that falls below such a support level has experienced insufficient demand to absorb whatever supply is out there, and so prices must fall to restore order. There is nothing fancier about it.

> When charts agree with the fundamentals, the combination can be powerful.

How one view can prevent making a big mistake

Let's look at a different example where one look at the charts kept investors out of trouble, even as analysts were starting to upgrade stocks as being good value.

On November 27, 2001, a major Wall Street firm issued a buy recommendation on JP Morgan Chase (see Chart 4.13). Logically, since the stock had fallen during the span of this chart alone from 70 to 40, it *should* have been a good value at that time.

Chart 4.13

But the market said otherwise. First and foremost, the bear market of 2000-2002 was still very much in force at the time. One look at the chart told investors that the market was not quite ready to turn around. The trend was down and the late 2001 bounce was halted at resistance – a price where supply of shares was likely to emerge as many investors saw an opportunity to "get out even". The stock lost another 25% from the date of the upgrade.

When the charts disagree with the fundamentals, or at least the analyst's interpretation of the fundamentals, it is usually a better idea to listen to the market.

2

Putting Charts To Work
For You

Remember, technical analysis and charting are all about making decisions and not making predictions. Keep the following in mind at all times:

- **We only have three choices for action – buy, sell or hold**

  Everything else supports making that decision.

- **Leave the prognosticating to the talking heads on television**

  Many a trader has been dead right about the future of the market yet still ended up bankrupt.

- **Be goal oriented**

  The real reason we invest is to make money. Trading does indeed have an element of fun, but there are a lot of financially less risky and physically more adrenaline pumping ways to have a good time.

Charts are your tools, not your magic bullet. Let's now put them to work!

5. Putting Stocks To The Technical Test

Next, we are going to run through the tools we've learned so far to see if the stocks in which we might be interested are technically sound. All of these tools are available to small investors for free on the Internet, so anyone can perform their own technical tests. We will also show how this set of techniques squares with the better-known fundamental analysis practiced by most analysts on Wall Street.

There will be no maths, and we'll limit the jargon to the bare minimum. What we want to do is:

1. Find obvious patterns and trends

2. Check an indicator or two

3. Compare current condition to others

As has been said several times already, there are five major categories of tools in a complete technical toolbox, and novice chartists need only to have a basic understanding of what they do.

The three basic goals of the tools

Rather than list them by jargon-laced names, here are the three basic goals of the tools.

1. Seeing where the stock is currently trading and figuring out how it got there

This is where we explore charting tools such as:

- *stock trends,*

- *support levels* (that point at which a stock is trading at which demand is thought to be strong enough to prevent the price from declining further), and

- *resistance levels* (that price at which selling is thought to be strong enough to prevent the price from rising further).

We'll also try to find a pattern or a trend to help.

2. Determining the power of a trend

This is also where we can find signs of an imminent end of a trend. For that, we will look at important technical concepts such as *trading volume* and *momentum.*

3. Making comparisons of the stock to the market, its peers in its own industry and even to its own history

This is where we look at relative performance and moving averages. We have not covered relative performance of a stock to its industry group yet, but it is simple enough to cover directly here.

If we know how fast a stock is moving, how much power is behind it and how it stacks up to the market, then we'll gain a huge advantage over other investors looking only at the fundamentals (such as price-to-earnings ratios, return on equity, or earnings growth).

A solid company with a solid chart is hard to beat.

Checklist for success

In looking at a stock, here is a checklist of key technical tools.

Any potential investment should meet most, but not necessarily all, of these criteria.

Price structure

Trends and trendlines

There is no secret to finding a trend. If prices are generally rising and making higher highs as well as higher lows, then we have a rising trend. Most charting web sites also offer the ability to draw trendlines on the chart to clearly define the trend more objectively. Alternatively, the old-fashioned way of printing the chart and using a ruler and pencil works just as well.

✓ We want stocks that are in rising trends.

Support and resistance

These are terms that simply tell us what price levels are likely to bring out the buyers (demand) or the sellers (supply), respectively.

✓ What we want to see is a current price that has either just moved through resistance (demand overwhelmed supply) or one that is far from the next resistance level.

Moving averages

Moving averages (or simply *price averages*) are just average prices over a user-defined period of time, usually 50 or 200 days. They help us determine if a trend is turning, as prices cross the averages. They also help us determine if an existing trend is progressing in an orderly manner, or if it is accelerating in a frenzy.

✓ Clearly, we are looking for prices to be above selected averages but not too far above them.

Relative performance

Relative performance charts simply divide the price of a stock by a relevant market index or industry group. The theory is that we should buy strong stocks in strong sectors and this is how we find them. If the ratio is going up, then the stock is outperforming the market or industry and is thus a strong candidate for further gains. If the ratio is going down, then the stock is lagging and is often more vulnerable to bad news.

✓ We are looking for stocks whose relative performance is increasing.

Volume

The number of shares traded and when those shares trade – either on days when prices rise or when they fall – can confirm the health of a trend or warn of an impending change.

✓ We are looking to see if buying is spreading to other investors and for urgency for all to buy when prices start to rise. Fear of missing a good thing causes these surges.

Momentum

Jargon alert! The next paragraph is summarized in one sentence at the end.

We also want to know if days when the stock rises outnumber those when it falls. Are the gains on these positive days greater than the losses on negative days? When the losing days are bigger and more frequent than the winning days we can surmise that the trend is weakening.

✓ We want to know if momentum is strong but not too euphoric.

Sentiment

We'll just worry about obvious extremes in sentiment, as this portion of the analysis is tricky even for the pros. Is everybody thinking the same thing? That's the time to go the other way. And as some traders will say, sometimes the best trades are the ones that make you sick as you leave the comfort of the crowd.

> Sometimes the best trades are the ones that make you sick as you leave the comfort of the crowd.

✓ We want to know if everyone is thinking the same thing.

OK, let's do it!

Now that we have the theory and the tools, let's look at the process of going from a stock idea to an actual decision to buy or sell.

1. Look at the trend

We want a rising trend or one that is just starting to do so.

2. Find nearby support and resistance levels

We are trying to find stocks where demand exceeds supply and new supply is not likely to develop soon.

3. Determine if the current trend is healthy

We want prices to be above a relevant moving average, but not so far that the stock is prone to a snapback decline as profit taking sets in.

4. Check volume and momentum indicators

We need to be sure that they are not fading as the stock price rises: A falling indicator warns that there might be technical problems before price action sours.

5. Find out if the stock is leading a benchmark

Is the particular stock at least matching the performance of the market and its peers?

If the stock passes at least three of these tests, we have a candidate for purchase.

A good candidate to buy

The chart coming up next is loaded with everything needed to make a decision to buy, sell or hold. As a result, it is very crowded. Do not let this scare you. When you look at your own charts it will not have all of the labels and symbols to clutter the view.

Hewlett-Packard is an example of a stock that passes these tests in 2006 (see Chart 5.1). It has a rising trend and when its October correction ended, it had a surge in price and volume as investors jumped in. Momentum readings were positive, the recent low did not violate the rising 50-day moving average, and prices were above a nicely rising 200-day average. Relative strength analysis shows it outperforming the market, and there is no meaningful resistance in sight.

Although the stock pulled back slightly after this chart was drawn, it went on to gain three points, or 7.5%, over the next two months. It may not have been the greatest move of all time but it was certainly pretty good. Hit enough singles like this and the home runs will take care of themselves.

Chart 5.1

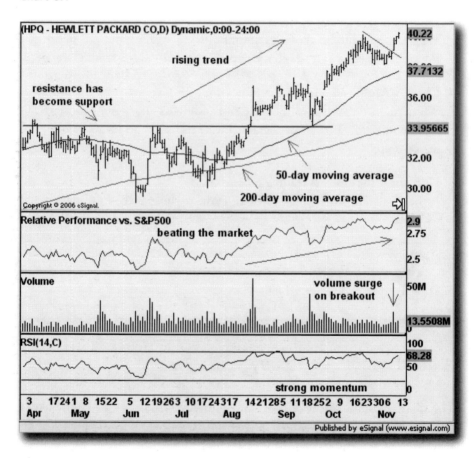

A good candidate to avoid

Lennar was an example of a stock that did not pass these tests (see Chart 5.2). After losing more than a quarter of its value as of the time the chart was drawn in 2007, some might think it was finally a cheap stock. However, the market was clearly saying quite the opposite.

Chart 5.2

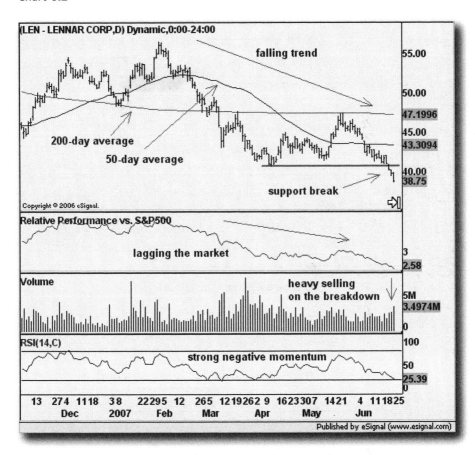

The trend was down, it was below its moving averages and it had just fallen below support on heavy volume and strong downside momentum. Not only that, it was falling as the market was rising! Over the next seven trading days, it was down 2.75 points, or an additional 7%. These are the kinds of losses the charts can easily help us avoid.

A stock that gets a "maybe"

In the real world, it is rare to find all technical ducks in a row, as we saw in the previous two charts, and that means we must make judgement calls about whether enough factors are in our favour.

Juniper Networks is an example of a stock that passed some tests but not enough of them to be a good buy candidate at that time (see Chart 5.3). On the positive side, it had a rising trend and had recently moved above a short-term resistance with a surge in volume (demand). It also bounced off both its 50-day and 200-day moving averages a month prior. Finally, it had been outperforming the market since August.

Chart 5.3

But there was a rather strong resistance just overhead at 20.50 from the peaks of March and April. At that time, the stock was licking its wounds following a disastrous seven-month performance that culminated in a one-day plunge. Bottom fishers were nibbling and investors who bought just prior to the plunge were looking at their chance to break even by selling near the pre-breakdown price. In other words, a good deal of supply was waiting to come into the market and that very same condition remained in place.

The strategy is to put this stock on the radar screen and watch how it reacts as it hits 20.50. If it powers through that level then we know the market has absorbed all that supply.

 Waiting to buy may give up a point or so of potential profit, but it reduces the risk of loss should the market be unable to soak up that supply.

What if you made a mistake?

Sometimes, no matter how full and unambiguous the analysis seems, an investment just doesn't work out. Charts are the only tools available to show this – and show it in a hurry.

The market is never wrong

No matter what the indicators might say, even if they all line up on one side of the argument, the market itself always has the final word. If we take an action and it results in a loss, we can never claim that the market made a wrong move. After all, we are trying to analyse what the market is doing. The market is not responsible for following the path we lay out for it.

In January 2007, the Standard & Poor's 500 Index had just dipped below an extremely clear rising trendline (see Chart 5.4). Momentum readings had been falling for weeks to signify that the rally was running out of power and, not shown on the chart, volume was starting to shrink. These signs together suggested that it was time to step aside and let the much-needed correction take place.

Chart 5.4

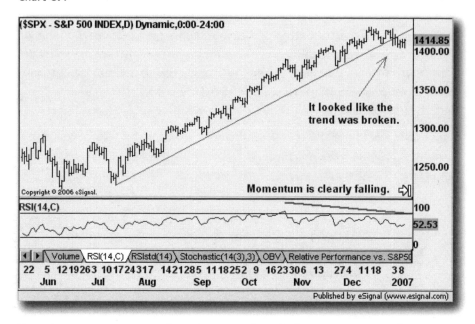

For whatever reason – and to chart watchers it does not matter what it is – the market rallied for another six weeks to fresh new highs.

Sometimes things just change

Conditions in the market are always changing, and sometimes a bad investment is just one of those unintended casualties. Perhaps a bank raised its prime lending rate, setting off a cascade of copycats and a reaction in the bond market. Interest rates go up and the stock market stumbles. Was that the fault of the investor? No. But it demands that the investor re-evaluate the charts and, if appropriate, sell stocks that have soured despite having solid technicals just one day earlier.

Ace Limited, a property and casualty insurer, provides just such an example (see Chart 5.5). It had already passed the technical tests outlined earlier, and on July 2 it broke out from a trading range. It was a fairly good signal that the stock was in good shape and ready for more gains.

But on July 5, the Bank of England raised its key short-term interest rate and the entire insurance sector fell sharply.

Why?

Again, for the charts it does not matter (but for those interested it was because insurance stocks such as this one typically hold large portfolios of bonds). Not only did a major central bank take action, but the bond market itself was already in decline to send interest rates to a one-year high. Clearly, conditions outside the stock market had changed and this stock should now be kept on a very tight leash to sell on any further price deterioration.

Chart 5.5

Sometimes the investor misreads the signs

Every investor, from novice to professional super-trader, makes mistakes. Perhaps they read something into the chart that really was not there. Maybe they read the charts with a preconceived idea of what the stock should do. And it is always possible to simply miss a detail.

When the stock drops, technical levels may be violated or stops are triggered. And that brings us to the next section on knowing when to sell. The pros know that the plan to sell is more important than the plan to buy. They know in advance what has to happen to cause them to throw in the towel and move on to something else.

> Every investor, from novice to professional super-trader, makes mistakes.

Knowing when to sell

One mistake made by many investors is not having a plan to sell what they have bought. Stocks, bonds and mutual funds are often put away in a portfolio and left there indefinitely, until either the bonds mature or the stocks and funds are sold at probate. For the latter, the rationale is that stocks return 10% or so over the long-term and therefore will be higher by that amount each year no matter what.

Of course, that sort of buy-and-hold-forever thinking caused investors to ride the bear market of 2000-2002 all the way down as some of their holdings lost 75-99% of their value. Even a blue-chip name such as JP Morgan Chase bank shed more than three quarters of its value during that span. Stocks, it seems, can indeed go down.

For professional money managers and individual investors alike, these are the reasons to sell a stock:

1. A calculated price objective was reached

2. The investment simply did not work out as planned and the risk/reward picture changed

3. Prices fell by a predetermined amount or percentage and selling at a loss would limit that loss to a small amount

All of these reasons are variations on the idea that we would not make a fresh purchase of the stock at its current price regardless of the price of the initial purchase.

Let's look at these three reasons in some detail.

1. Price objective reached

If we buy a stock believing that it will rise 25% over two years from whatever analysis we use and it meets that goal, we should take our profits and move on. The only reason to hold on longer is if the charts and other analyses say that there is a second price objective likely to be met. In other words, we would buy it at the current price if we did not already own it.

2. The investment did not perform

We do not want to hold on to a stock forever hoping that it will finally start to go up. We also do not want to hold on to a stock that develops negative chart patterns or fundamental problems before it reaches its objective. Just because analysis said it was good does not mean it will do what we want.

3. Stopped out

A stop is a price level at which we give up and admit we made a mistake. We cut our losses, stop the financial bleeding and move on to something better. Does this bruise the ego? Sure it does, but ego is not how money is made. Leave your ego at home and honour your analysis objectively. This old saw bears repeating: *'All big losses begin as small losses.'*

> A stop is a price level at which we give up and admit we made a mistake.

> If we know what has to happen to cause us to sell then we reduce a lot of uncertainty. We'll sleep better, too, knowing that risk is being controlled.

How about the fundamentals?

At this point, we must revisit how fundamental analysis and technical analysis can have different conclusions about the same stock.

For example, a stock that has strong technicals may be overvalued based on the fundamentals. Conversely, a stock may seem cheap based on the fundamentals, while technicians are selling it because it failed to meet many of the tests cited above.

> There will be times when the market sees things the fundamental analyst does not see.

This is not a problem with either method as there will be times when the market sees things the fundamental analyst does not see.

There will also be times the fundamental analyst knows something about the company that is being overwhelmed by some non company-specific news. An example might be a positive earnings forecast on a day when a peer stock releases bad news that sends the entire sector lower.

When both fundamentals and technicals line up, investors can buy with confidence. But even when they don't line up, simply being aware of risks from either side empowers investors to make better decisions.

6. Technical Analysis In Action

This section covers the next level in understanding how to use charts – yet still keeps it to its simplest forms. Understanding the concepts in a technical analysis classroom is great, but when we can find it in the real world and use that to help make our decisions to buy, sell or hold, then we really have a powerful tool at our disposal.

What is going on around you?

Charts help us understand the psychology of the market, from fear to greed and from apathy to obsession. They also show us when the herd is stampeding and we should join along. They also show us when that herd is going to run right off a cliff and we should get out of the way.

Technical analysis can help gauge how happy people are in the market. Normally, happy people invest in stocks and unhappy people tend to shun them; most of the time, the correlations of happy to bullish and unhappy to bearish ring true. However, there are times when people can be so bullish that it becomes bad for the market.

When people believe that stocks can do no wrong, they increase their appetite for risk. They pay less attention to the details of their investments because they believe that buying a stock at 50 or 51 is

> There are times when people can be so bullish that it becomes bad for the market.

the same thing when they expect 15% gains each year. The market will bail them out of any poorly timed trades or stocks with marginal fundamentals.

But we all know that does not last.

When basic investment principles and – we'll borrow from the fundamentals – basic measures of a company's health are ignored, we know the market is overheated. The companies may still be great but people are paying far too much for their stocks. Sooner or later, the market will self-correct. They say:

But this time it is different!

It is never different.

The process of investing may change but the forces driving the market do not. They bend but they will return to normal. Charts help us figure out when perception and reality get too far out of line.

What do you see on the charts?

If we strip away all the fancy analysis, what is left is the trend of the stock, index or commodity. If the trend is up we want to own it. If it is down we do not want to own it. For most investors, there is a simple mantra to follow:

Up is good, down is bad.

This is trite, to be sure, but it is all that really matters when it comes to investing. We want to buy something with a good chance that it will be higher in price when we are ready to sell it, whether that be next week, next year or when we retire.

Some trends are smooth and it is easy to identify their existence. Others are erratic and timing becomes more crucial. Still others, such as the coffee market was in 2000, have smooth trends interrupted by occasional bouts of insanity (see Chart 6.1).

Chart 6.1

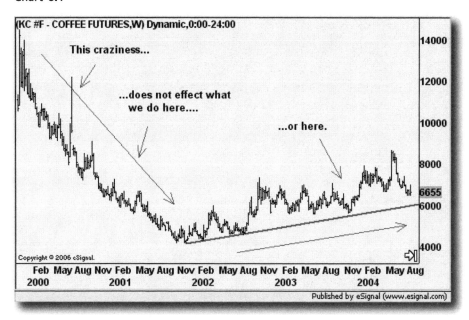

Don't let the fact that this is a commodity chart scare you. A trend is a trend no matter what asset class it covers.

But the key point is to find a stock or commodity where prices are generally rising.

Sometimes there just isn't anything there

There are times when technical analysis will not be able to decipher the market's message. Perhaps a pattern is too irregular or too vague. Certainly, analysis of a stock with low trading volume or a very thin float (shares outstanding) cannot be as reliable, because by definition technical analysis seeks to measure the psychology of the crowd. That demands that there be a crowd (participation by the public) and the liquidity it brings.

Further, a stock embroiled in legal battles, takeover activity or geopolitical problems is going to be rocked by news events and not by normal market forces. There is no shame in avoiding these securities simply because market forces are taking a back seat to other forces.

Chart 6.2

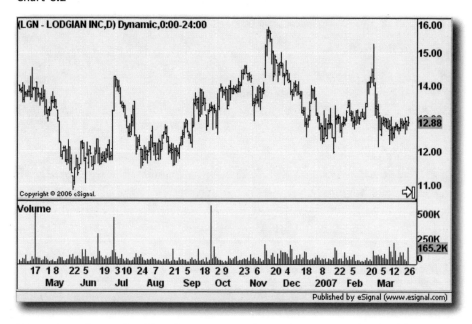

Not only is the stock of hotel operator Lodgian showing no discernible trends or patterns, it also trades relatively low values each day (see Chart 6.2).

A combination of low price and low volume makes analysis here much less reliable, so forcing patterns on the chart is clearly not a good idea.

> With literally thousands of stocks from which to choose, there is no reason to force analysis on any one of them. Find something else where the technical evidence is much more compelling.

The real world

A key objective of this book is to introduce the reader to a tool which will either confirm or refute other forms of analysis, from a broker recommendation to the consensus opinion in an investment club. The following charts overlay highly paid analyst opinions on price action, and show that it is not always a good idea to follow those opinions blindly.

Again, it is not fundamental analysis that is flawed or even the analyst's ability to use it. Rather, we are just checking to see what the market itself thinks about the stock in question and acting accordingly.

Uncommon values?

Market analysts are often considered to be smart people – and indeed most are. However, nobody is as smart as the market itself, so a sanity check on analysts' recommendations is certainly a good idea.

Here are charts following the release of a major brokerage house's top recommended list for the year beginning in June 2001, and again for the year beginning in June 2003. Cisco Systems was on both lists and we can see that it was a fair winner in 2003-2004, but a net loser in 2001-2002 (see Chart 6.3).

Chart 6.3

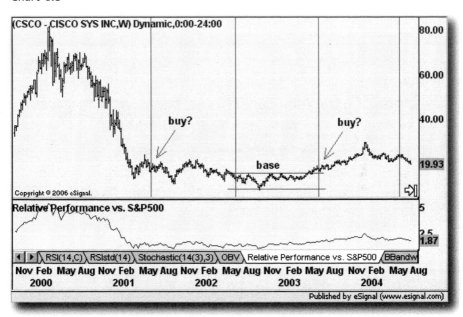

In 2001, the trend was still down and there was nothing fancy about the chart analysis. The market did not agree with the fundamental analyst, in this case.

However, in 2003, the stock had been trading sideways to form a trading range, or a base, and arguably had emerged from that base just before the second recommended list was released. The market said that things had changed for the better, agreeing with the analysts.

Another stock recommended in 2001 was Alcoa, which had just enjoyed a nice multi-month rally (see Chart 6.4). But just before the list was published, the stock broke down hard and moved below its rising trendline. In other words, the market was saying that things had changed and it was time to cash in. It went on to be a decent loser over the following year.

Chart 6.4

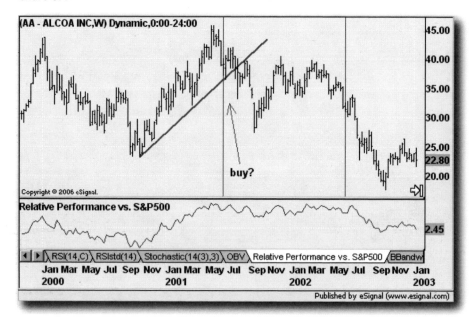

Amgen was on the list in 2003, and while it was moving well just after the list was released, there was a fairly substantial resistance zone not far above (see Chart 6.5). The risk/reward equation was low.

Chart 6.5

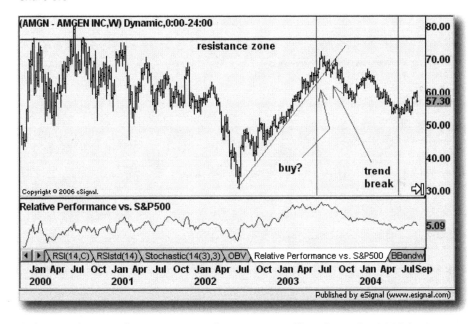

A few weeks into the investment, the rising trendline from the 2002 low was broken and the market gave a clear signal that downside risk was significantly elevated. It was clearly time to get out.

Journalists know better?

One of the major financial magazines ran an article praising Pharmaceutical Product Development in June 2002, with all sorts of justifications as to why it was a good investment (see Chart 6.6). Although it does not look like much visually on the chart shown here, over the next few short weeks the stock shed more than a third of its value. While it did bounce back from there, the damage was done to the portfolio, requiring a 50% rally just to break even. Further, the stock went nowhere for the next two years.

Chart 6.6

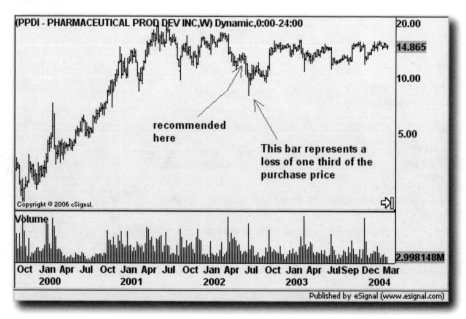

Here's what a technician saw

The same chart with a few basic tools applied reveals the market telling us very clearly that this stock was in some trouble (see Chart 6.7). One year later, the price of the stock had recovered, but it took over two years before the stock emerged from a trendless state to finally turn a significant profit. The charts should have kept investors out of this time and opportunity-wasting investment.

Chart 6.7

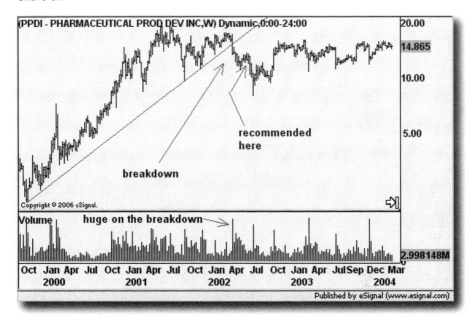

Upgrades and downgrades – but did they make us any money?

International Business Machines presents a great case for letting the market tell us what to do and not Wall Street analysts (see Chart 6.8).

There are two analyst upgrades on this chart (captioned in grey) that had value for investors. But following the advice of the upgrades and downgrades captioned in black were either money losers, or at a minimum profit wasters.

In January 2005, just after an analyst upgrade, the stock fell apart. And where were the three analysts who downgraded the stock in April months earlier before their clients' profits evaporated?

Chart 6.8

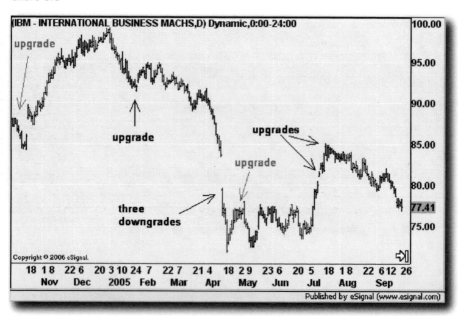

What a technician saw

The chart watcher saw a bullish breakout pattern in October 2004, a bearish breakdown in March 2005, and a basing pattern with breakout in July 2005 (see Chart 6.9). Not drawn on the chart to avoid clutter is a trendline from the December 2004 peak, that suggested the breakout from the base would run into some trouble.

Chart 6.9

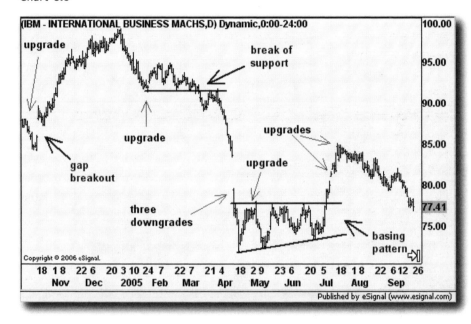

Don't be afraid of high prices

While it is great to buy low and sell high, more often we should try to buy stocks that have already proven that they can rally. We *buy high* and *sell higher* to capture the bulk of a gain but not all of it. Let's leave the extra few points – and their associated risk – to the professionals.

Chart 6.10

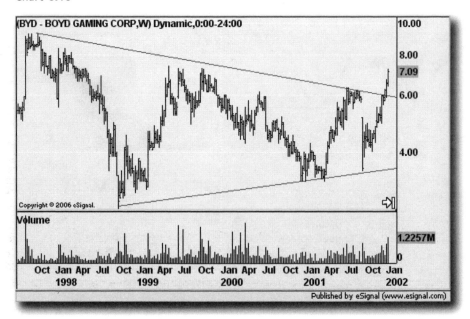

Boyd Gaming broke through a resistance line as 2002 got underway, but investors could have been reasonably unnerved enough not to buy it there (see Chart 6.10). After all, the stock had rallied from below 4.0 to the breakout point of 6.0 in a short period of time, and a 50% gain seems like more than enough to expect. (Note: This chart is drawn with a semi-logarithmic scale to show percent price changes.)

The market is speaking!

But the stock never looked back and tripled from that original breakout buy signal (see Chart 6.11). Note how once again it broke higher from a resistance line in early 2004 with healthy volume.

Chart 6.11

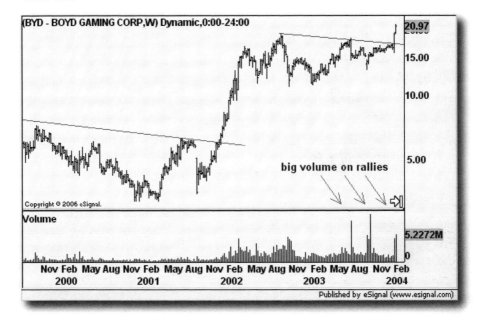

The market peaked before the news hit

From that second breakout point, the stock tripled again in a little more than a year, peaking in April 2005, five months before Hurricane Katrina devastated the Gulf Coast of the US and destroyed a good deal of Boyd's business. (see Chart 6.12). Did the market know a hurricane was coming? Of course not, but the market was already signalling that the conditions were changing and any shocks would be met with selling.

When the trendline finally broke in September 2005, in the wake of the hurricane, long-term investors knew it was time to cash in their winnings. The stock was unlikely to have the strength to recover quickly.

Of course, by that point, the stock had dropped considerably. Shorter-term analysis would have picked up a breakdown several months earlier, to give even long-term investors a suggestion to take at least some of their money off the table and lock in a nice gain.

Chart 6.12

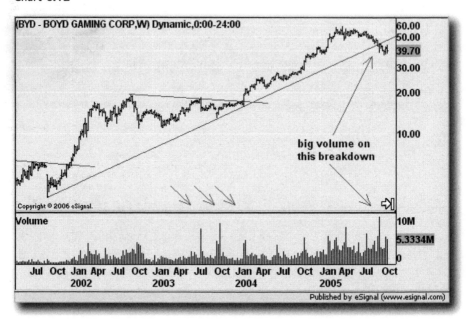

Preservation of capital

Here is a chart familiar to anyone following the news scandals of the post-bubble era.

Enron was trading in a wide range for more than a year before it began its death spiral on the charts (see Chart 6.13). Support at the 65-level was very clear and even if investors rode the stock down from the peak near 90, the charts gave an unmistakable line in the sand that was clearly crossed. The horizontal support line is drawn to drive home the point about extreme danger for investors, as it was broken.

Chart 6.13

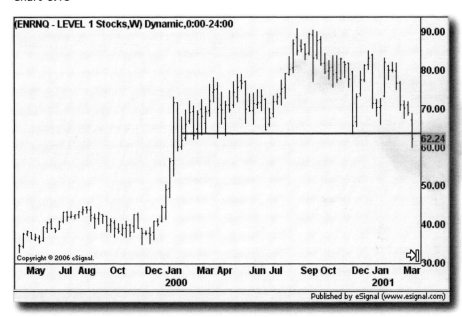

Again, short-term analysis would have yielded clues to get out even earlier, but for even casual long-term investors, there was no reason to lose it all as the company fell into disgrace.

Chart 6.14

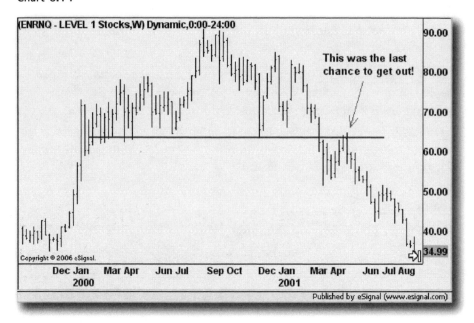

What is great about the way this stock traded, was that in April 2001 it rallied as analysts clamoured over each other to issue reassuring reports and buy recommendations (see Chart 6.14). Investors missing the opportunity to get out at 65 had their second chance to do so. Support had become resistance, as it so often does in all markets.

The real reason we do this

Market analysis leads to one goal – making the buy, sell or hold decision. Investing is all about making money and not looking smart. Leave your ego at the door because trying to out-do the next person, or save face after making a bad decision, will cost even more money than has already been lost.

This is not about predicting the future. Knowing where a stock, or the overall market, will be in a year or two would be great, but we cannot control that. All we can do is own stocks or not own them, and that means deciding what to do right now.

Leave the predictions to the psychics. We want to make money.

7. When The Real World Does Not Follow The Script

Sometimes things do not work as planned.

Sometimes we need to use a bit of fudging or, to put it a bit more professionally, make some judgement calls. It is rare that we see textbook set-ups and if we wait for everything to fall into place we will miss opportunities. Call that *analysis paralysis*.

Technicians license

The debate continues on whether technical analysis is an art or a science. Those of the latter belief work with equations, trading systems and models. Those of the former belief use trendlines, traditional technical patterns and an experienced eye. Just like writers who use journalistic license to bend the rules of grammar and facts, market technicians selectively ignore various chart points, to create a meaningful and, more importantly, useful analysis.

Rationale

Strict interpretation of technical rules can cause the technician to set seemingly accurate support and resistance levels that are weak and not related to true market conditions. A daily chart of ExxonMobil in 2004, shows a very useful trend channel and trading range with multiple violations of what might be considered strict rules of pattern construction (see Chart 7.1). Each violation is marked with an arrow.

The rising channel, which is simply a trendline and a companion parallel line drawn to contain the action, was violated several times above and below its borders. But because the lines are drawn where they are, they describe the action over the life of the chart much better than if they had been drawn to capture every bit of data.

Chart 7.1

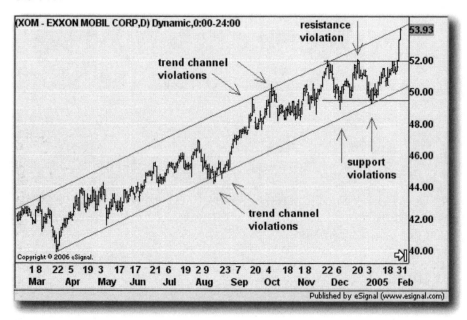

Similarly, the trading range seen late in the year was drawn with four of its five peaks and troughs in violation of its borders. Even with 80% of its defining points seemingly incorrect, the result was a very clear trading range that allowed nimble investors to spot its breakout early and get in for maximum profit.

 Spending too much time deciding which price to use in a trading system or model can let profitable trades slip away.

By using a range of prices instead of a single price, or choosing to ignore outlying data, extreme intraday reactions can be ignored. This automatically places greater significance on the close or cluster of trading in the market analysed.

What makes sense?

Unlike regression analysis, where a line is drawn to represent all the data, fitting a trading channel to the market places support and resistance trendlines at levels that correspond to the majority of significant highs and lows.

A weekly chart of AT&T shows a rally beginning in late 2006, and a technically correct trendline can be drawn from that point (see Chart 7.2).

Chart 7.2

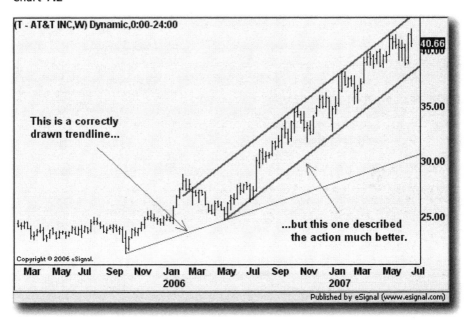

After all, the textbook dictates that trendlines be drawn from the starting point of a rally and through the first significant pullback. But that trendline here would essentially be meaningless. It certainly was of no help in 2006-2007, in determining whether we should buy, sell or hold the stock.

However, by using the next significant low as the start of the trendline, not only can a meaningful trend be identified, but a parallel line (forming a trend channel) can be added to contain the rally. Buying at pullbacks to the line and selling at touches of the parallel line would have created short-term opportunities for traders, at the same time giving long-term investors confidence to hold on.

Variations

Chart reading has always been considered an interpretive skill and often cannot be tamed by mechanical systems. Even the latest innovations in setting trendlines and price targets still cannot substitute for the human mind in leaving room for variations of traditional patterns.

Let's take a look at a pattern that is "close enough" to the textbook version and see that the spirit of the pattern, if not its strict construction, was indeed in place.

Abercrombie & Fitch was in a nice rally in late 2004 when it stalled (see Chart 7.3).

Chart 7.3

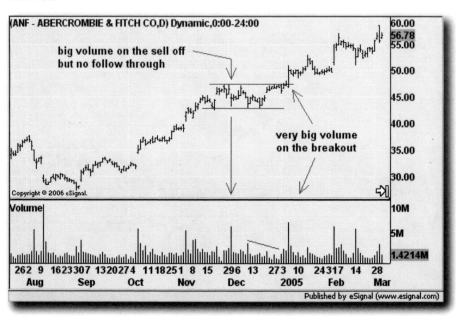

On December 2 of that year, there was a sudden sell-off with heavy volume traded, and normally that should have kicked off a new declining trend. Owning the stock at the time was not supposed to be a good idea.

But there was no follow-through to the selling day, suggesting that all the supply which was going to swamp the market did not materialize. Prices moved sideways for weeks until January 6, 2005, when the stock broke out to the upside with even heavier volume.

The spirit of a trading range or rectangle pattern such as this, is a pause in a trend that allows investors to rethink their positions. Volume is supposed to fade, as it did here, as uncertainty builds. Prices tend to cycle from the top of the pattern to the bottom, if not in a regular manner but at least in an identifiable one.

For Abercrombie, prices hugged the upper border for almost two weeks, which is in violation of the cyclical nature of trading within a pattern but, as can be seen in the chart, there were enough of these cycles to create a spirit of uncertainty and of waiting for something to happen. That something is a move either above or below the pattern – in this case we see a very clear breakout.

One look at the chart should have said that this stock was ready to rally some more.

Johnson & Johnson presented a triangle-like pattern in late 2006-early 2007, that clearly violated the rules of pattern construction (see Chart 7.4).

Chart 7.4

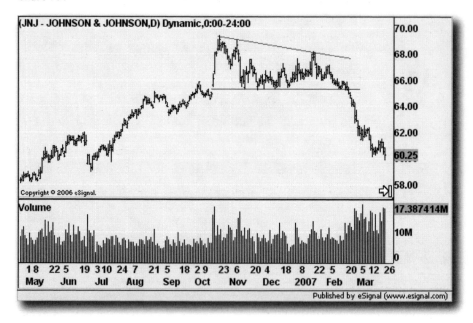

There were few swings from pattern bottom to pattern top, especially during the middle part of the pattern, and there was no cyclical motion at all. Yet, the stock showed a very clear support level at 65.30, where investors came in to buy what they thought were cheap shares.

When that level was broken to the downside in February 2007, volume surged. Supply beat demand and prices continued much lower. Anyone owing the stock got a very unmistakable signal to get out.

This was a triangle pattern because trading became choppy and each significant rally attempt, though irregular, failed at lower levels. The spirit of the pattern was a pause after a nice rally and October 2006 surge that transitioned the stock from bull to bear.

Let the market talk

Most novice technical analysts, and probably a few experienced ones, look at a chart with preconceived notions about what the market will do. This usually narrows the analysis and often provides incorrect results. The bottom line is that you cannot impose your will on the market and that means waiting until the market tells you what to do. It also means continuing to listen in case it changes its mind.

Finding order

Some charts, like those of the major stock markets, seem to travel up or down for long periods of time. Finding the trend there is easy. Likewise, when chart patterns are crisp, textbook versions, knowing what to do about them is also straightforward.

But most of the time, trends and patterns are not so clear. The idea is to let the patterns emerge without applying too many indicators and literally squinting your eyes at the screen in the hope that your brain can create order from the jumble of data before you.

The chart of Archer Daniels Midland in 2004 looked like a clutter of lines and noise (see Chart 7.5). But there are a few observations that even a beginner can make, including the overall trend and the stock's habit of making false moves before getting a trend moving.

Look at the chart for a minute and see if anything jumps out at you.

Chart 7.5

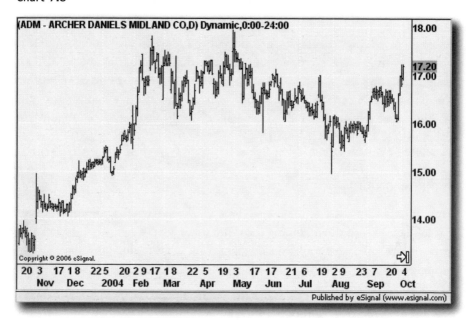

With two quick lines, the strength of this stock became evident (see Chart 7.6).

Chart 7.6

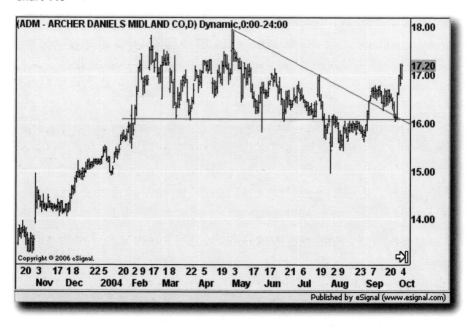

A support level was broken in July but the stock held its ground anyway. The subsequent rally broke a trendline, albeit a weak one, and the dip that followed tested both the trendline and the old support. This stock was a buy right here and it rallied to 25 within five months. That's a 45% gain over the winter.

Don't force it

Forcing lines on the chart is the same as telling the market to follow the path you outline rather than finding the lines the market gives you to follow.

 If you have difficulty finding trends and patterns it is better not to buy or sell and to move on to something else. We cannot figure out what to do with every stock so let's just stick to the ones that the market gives us.

Summary – the real world

Technical analysis is based on the premise that price patterns repeat themselves. This is because people in the markets repeat themselves given similar market conditions.

Unfortunately, in the real world, the term "similar market conditions" is subject to interpretation. It's important that we can give patterns some leeway in their development and understand what to do when things "sort of" happen.

The patterns we examined in this chapter were imperfect and constitute the majority of patterns we'll encounter. The key is to be able to see the bigger picture of what is going on with any stock or market and understand what the public is thinking as these patterns are created.

- Are the bulls taking profits?

- Are the bears taking advantage of high prices by aggressively selling?

Technical patterns are rarely crystal clear because some market participants do not wait until they complete before acting. This forces patterns to distort slightly even though the general meaning is not changed.

8. Examples

This chapter is the workbook portion of the book and presents many chart examples. Try to form an opinion on your own before reading the text for each.

Chart 8.1

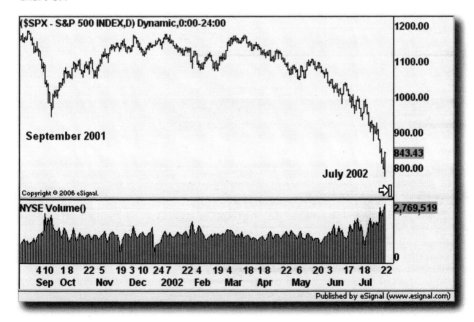

The Standard & Poor's 500 is shown here at the end of the bear market of 2000-2002 (see Chart 8.1). On the left of the chart is the steep decline leading to, and following, the September 11 attacks. Volume during that decline surged to panic levels and the implications from the price and volume data alone suggested extreme pessimism. Investors were selling stock with abandon with a "get me out at any price" mentality.

That marked a temporary bottom, but in 2002 the index sagged once again. In July of that year once again, price action accelerated its decline and volume surged to levels above even the post-September 11 panic, and that marked the absolute end to the bear market. Although the market continued to lick its wounds for several more months, it was time to start looking for stocks to buy, not sell.

Jargon alert! For the more advanced reader, note the bullish reversal bar at the very end of the chart. People went from panic selling to urgent buying within a single day, further confirming that an important bottom had been made.

Chart 8.2

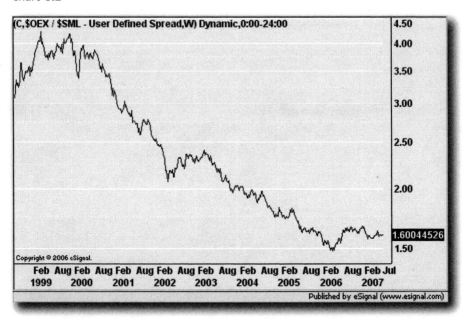

Chart 8.2 is a long-term chart comparing the performance of big stocks to small stocks. It is a simple ratio of the price of the S&P 100 "biggest cap" index and the S&P 600 small cap index. When the ratio is rising, big stocks are outperforming small stocks but, as we can see here, the small caps were the winners for several years.

What do you see here? (Answer on next chart.)

Chart 8.3

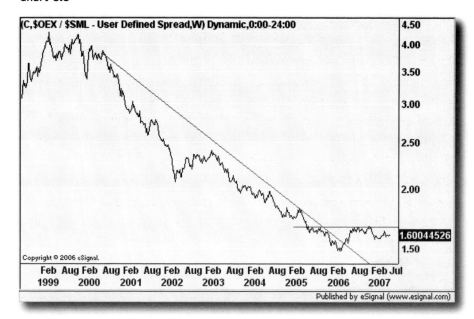

Something happened in mid 2006 to end that dominance, and small stocks were no longer the *de facto* market leaders anymore (see Chart 8.3). To be sure, big stocks have not yet taken the lead as of the time this chart was drawn. One test to see if big stocks have truly taken the lead would be a break of the resistance line connecting the tops seen in 2005 and 2006. If that occurs, then we can shift investment strategies to favour the new leaders.

Chart 8.4

In this chart (8.4), the Philadelphia Stock Exchange gold and silver stock index had broken free from a trading range in late 2005, and rallied quite well. But in 2006, it began to trade higher and lower in a choppy pattern with a support line that was drifting lower. In October 2006, when this chart ends, the support line and the top of the former trading range had converged to create a very likely place to find demand heating up for the sector. Within weeks, the index was back near the upper end of its new pattern.

Jargon alert! The more advanced reader will note that the new pattern was a head-and-shoulders, so support at the convergence of the former trading range top and sloping support line was critical. A breakdown there would have had negative implications for months to come.

Chart 8.5

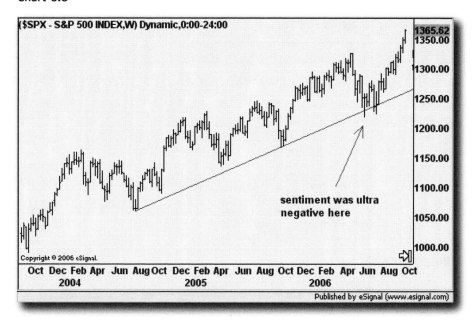

($SPX - S&P 500 INDEX,W) Dynamic,0:00-24:00

1365.62
1350.00
1300.00
1250.00
1200.00
1150.00
1100.00
1050.00
1000.00

sentiment was ultra negative here

Copyright © 2006 eSignal.

Oct Dec Feb Apr Jun Aug Oct Dec Feb Apr Jun Aug Oct Dec Feb Apr Jun Aug Oct
2004   2005   2006

Published by eSignal (www.esignal.com)

In Chart 8.5, the S&P 500 had violated its rising trendline twice in the summer of 2006, yet it did not actually break down. Any investor keeping tabs on all aspects of charting, including sentiment, would have had an idea that something was out of line at that time. People were so bearish, and we learned from surveys of investor attitudes, newsletter writer consensus and even the abundance of put options over call options being bought, that we had to demand the market make a much clearer break down to believe it. As we can see here, the market rocketed into new high ground, fuelled by all the doubters that were slowly drawn back into the market and increasing demand.

Chart 8.6

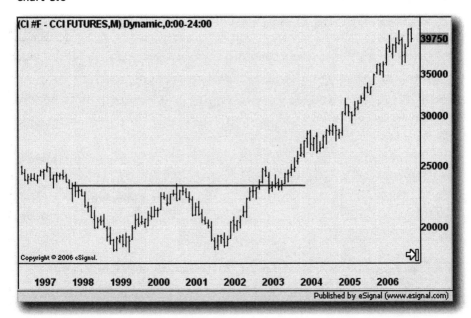

The Commodities Research Bureau index of commodities prices (original version) formed a (jargon alert!) *double bottom* pattern, so named because it has two troughs at the same price level (Chart 8.6). This pattern is simply a shortened trading range and when the upper border is broken, a new rising trend is confirmed. The sheer size of the pattern, taking place over several years, gave investors an idea that the bull market in commodities was going to last for quite some time – and they were right.

Chart 8.7

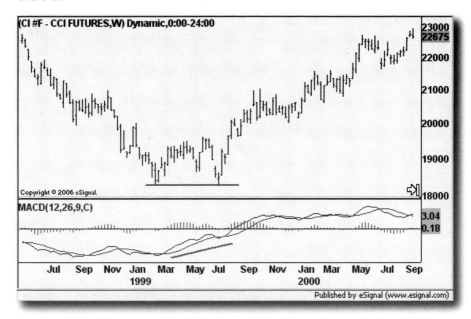

Here is a close-up of the first bottom seen in the previous chart, and it is also a double bottom pattern but on a smaller scale (Chart 8.7). A momentum indicator has been added. (It is the MACD again but it could be any momentum indicator you choose.) In July 1999, as the index came down to meet its January low, the momentum indicator failed to do the same. The divergence between indicator and price is a good tip-off that the bearish trend was ending and investors should be on the alert for the start of a new rising trend. That trend was confirmed when price moved above the May peak, breaking resistance.

Chart 8.8

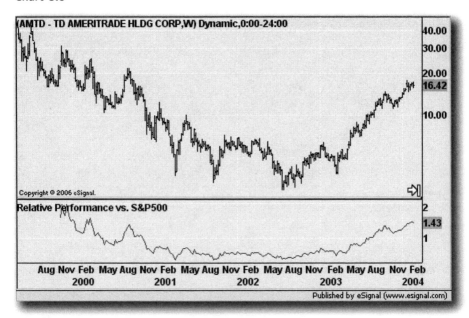

In Chart 8.8, we see TD Ameritrade falling during the bear market and then rising as the new bull market unfolded.

But what do we really see here and when should we have done something about it? (Answer on next chart.)

Chart 8.9

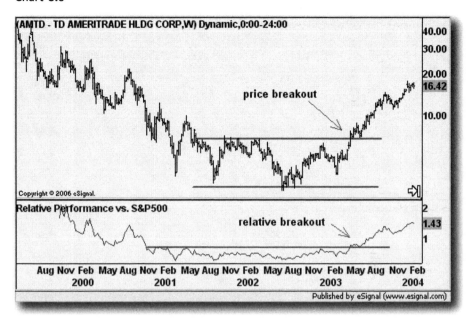

Chart 8.9 has a trading range, or basing pattern, drawn and we can see a clear breakout in 2003. Further, just before the price breakout, the stock scored a relative performance breakout vs. the broad market. These two signs made this stock one to own and we can see that it returned a nice profit, even to those investors who waited for these long-term signals to trigger.

Chart 8.10

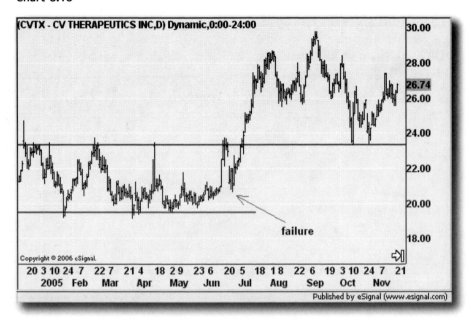

CV Therapeutics was in a nice trading range in early 2005, trading from pattern top to bottom and back again several times (Chart 8.10). However, in June it failed to trade back to the lower border. Something was different and it caused bulls to get aggressive at a higher price than had been the case previously. That was a warning to be on the alert for a breakout from the pattern itself.

What would be the plan now, given the support and resistance levels drawn here? (Answer on next chart.)

Chart 8.11

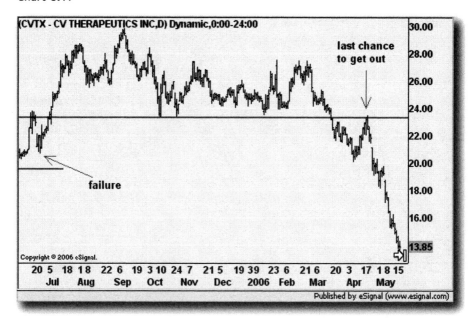

The stock settled into a new higher range with support (the bottom of the range) at the old resistance level (the top of the old range). When prices dipped below that level, it was time to get out. The market was kind here as a short rally gave those who missed it another chance to sell before the real damage set in. Look back at the Enron chart on page 106. Eerily similar.

Chart 8.12

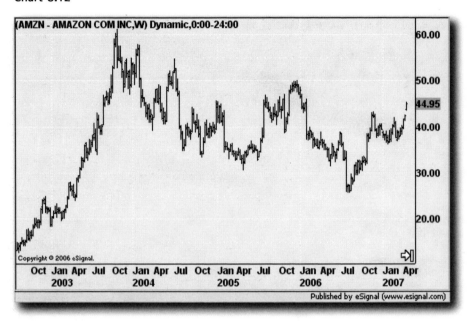

This weekly view of Amazon.com (Chart 8.12) shows a rather choppy declining trend but an interesting development in April 2007.

What should we do? (Answer on next chart.)

Chart 8.13

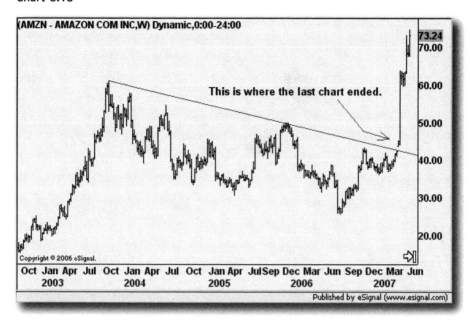

The charts told us something was happening in the last chart, but not what it was or how big it was going to be. In Chart 8.13, we see the result of a surprise earnings report and its aftermath. Clearly, this was a little lucky in terms of actual profit, but what was not luck at all was the chart telling us that we should own this stock on the trendline breakout. The rest was a gift.

9. Conclusion

Mention technical analysis at most mutual fund shops or university settings and it will be dismissed as being akin to consulting an oracle to make investment decisions. Many people consider fundamental analysis as the only method to determine whether a stock is under – or overvalued. They think that technical analysis tries to predict the future based on past performance, and as they paint in the fine print of their advertising disclaimers:

Past performance is no guarantee of future results.

Technical analysts will concur.

Charts do not predict the future from the past. They seek to find current buying and selling patterns in the past and plan their own course of action once those patterns end. It is based on probabilities, not forecasting.

Why does this work?

Because, as mentioned earlier, chart patterns are formed by the buying and selling actions of people, and people tend to act in a similar manner when faced with similar situations.

Some blame this on a self-fulfilling prophecy: if enough investors believe in the significance of a chart pattern ending then they will act, and thus their actions will assure that the assumed result will occur.

But investors may not act the same way this time and the charts will tell us when that is the case quickly, before losses begin to mount. Note that technical analysis expects to have losses. It is in minimizing those losses and recognizing when a winner has more room to go that there is success – read consistent profits – in a portfolio.

No other method of analysis includes as a standard feature the possibility that things will not work out as planned.

Wouldn't it have been great to know in December 2000 that a bear market had begun earlier in the year, with September 2000 as the last straw that broke the bull's back?

It certainly was better than riding the bear market lower and waiting for the fundamentals to deteriorate before selling out.

Charts need not be adversarial with other forms of analysis. Indeed, this book is focused on introducing charts as a tool to help with the other forms. Whether it is a sanity check on the fundamentals, or something that tips us off on changing fundamentals in a sector, charts will enhance investing results.

Charts are tools, not crystal balls. They help investors find good investments and just as importantly avoid bad ones. As they say, a picture is worth a thousand words and charts put that old saw into action to help investors make and keep money.

Index

Y

Yahoo Inc. 42

Z

zones, resistance 97